Ordering the African imagination
essays on culture and literature

Related titles

H. Otokunefor & O. Nwodo (eds), *Nigerian Female Writers: A critical perspective*
Tanure Ojaide, *The Poetry of Wole Soyinka*
Tayo Olafioye, *The Poetry of Tanure Ojaide: A critical appraisal*
Kanchana Ugbabe, *Chukwuemeka Ike: A critical reader*

Ordering the African imagination
essays on culture and literature

by

Tanure Ojaide

malthouse

Malthouse Press Limited
Lagos, Benin, Ibadan, Jos, Oxford, Zaria

Malthouse Press Limited
43 Onitana Street, Off Stadium Hotel Road
Surulere, Lagos
E-mail: malthouse_press@yahoo.com
malthouse_lagos@yahoo.co.uk
Tel: +234 (01) -773 53 44; 0802 364 2402

All rights reserved. No part of this publication may be reproduced, transmitted, transcribed, stored in a retrieval system or translated into any language or computer language, in any form or by any means, electronic, mechanical, magnetic, chemical, thermal, manual or otherwise, without the prior consent in writing of Malthouse Press Limited, Lagos, Nigeria.

This book is sold subject to the condition that it shall not by way of trade, or otherwise, be lent, re-sold, hired out, or otherwise circulated without the publisher's prior consent in writing, in any form of binding or cover other than in which it is published and without a similar condition, including this condition, being imposed on the subsequent purchaser.

© Tanure Ojaide 2007
First Published 2007
ISBN 978 023 204 4

Distributors:
African Books Collective Ltd
Email: abc@africanbookscollective.com
Website: http://www.africanbookscollective.com

Acknowledgements

Thanks to Lynne Rienner Publishers in whose *Sacred Spaces and Public Quarrels* (1999), edited by Ezekiel Kalipeni and Paul T. Zeleza, 'The Niger Delta, Nativity, and My Writing," first appeared. Thanks are also due to *The Guardian* of Nigeria in which "The Challenges of the African Writer Today" first appeared.

Preface

This book is an assembly of essays and lectures written and delivered respectively at different times in the past decade. They address issues of culture and literature from a personal African perspective. Some points are repeated in several essays to reinforce the overall concern about the plight of modern African culture with its literature. Being both a creative writer and a literary scholar, culture has always interested me. The two essays on African culture – the possible impact of the New World Order and globalization on African culture and the contemporary state of the culture – register this concern.

In each of these presentations, now chapters, I have worked from the premise that literature is a cultural production and so it has its unique aesthetics and other characteristics as the culture conditions both its creation and reception. What one culture considers good literature may not necessarily be seen as such in another culture. Culture conditions a writer's assumptions of his or her role (or none at all) as a writer. This inevitably results in the writer's fashioning a concept that governs the content and form of his or her writing. Put in a different way, there is a cultural tradition of literature and each writer or verbal artist fashions his work to enhance, subvert, or transform that tradition with his individual talent. The tradition provides the aesthetics with which to judge the success or otherwise of a literary creation.

The African writer in English, French, or Portuguese works within two cultures or traditions: the metropolitan culture of the language and the native/indigenous culture in which the African writer was raised and from which he or she writes. While no serious critic nowadays considers the African writing in an originally European language European literature, still the African writer has to be cognizant of being raised in one culture and writing in the vehicle of an alien culture. This has been more so since the language has been used as a tool in the domination of his or her people. One of the chapters, "Whose English?: The African Writer and the Language Issue," addresses a concern that has been there from the beginning of modern African literature. Many African writers respond individually and the now familiar positions of Chinua Achebe and Ngugi wa Thiongo reflect their respective acceptance or rejection of the foreign language as a vehicle for modern Africans to express themselves creatively.

Many African writers use the foreign-derived language, which has become extra-territorial and indigenized, to express their responses to contemporary reality. One could argue that much as the African writer, especially poet, attempts to be creative with the language of choice, he or she aims more to convey the sense of urgency of the African condition than to solely advance the language. While style stands out in a writer like Kojo Laing, the focus seems to be the content. For most African writers though, there is the attempt to balance content and form. Put differently, the content conditions the form of the literary work.

The focus of this book is African culture and its imaginative productions in the arts, especially in literature. One essay, "How the Urhobo people see the world through art," delves into plastic/visual art to reinforce the place of artistic productions in the lives of an African group. Art expresses the totality of the people's experience, worldview, and sensibility. In other words, the African creative imagination reflects the daily lives, beliefs, struggles, and the existential angst of the African people. No aspect of the people's experience is excluded; hence no material – political, social, economic, religious, or any other – is extra-literary to the African writer. Art reflects life just as life informs artistic creations. In the essay on "divine mentoring," an artistic tradition is exposed in the manner poetry, in the form of songs, was (and is still) composed by an African group and the place of religion and beliefs in the social consciousness and the artist's effort to create a healthy ethos in the community.

The essays derive from my concern about the direction of African culture and its artistic creations in a global age. The African writer has the right to write as he or she pleases, but it is important to know the tradition from which one writes. Since culture is dynamic, one expects the writer and scholar, even within one's culture, to be flexible in aesthetic choices by embracing some conventions and discarding others that are constrictive and inimical to humanity. Correspondingly, an African writer may absorb techniques or conventions that may help him or her create the new African reality. Relevance should be a guiding principle. The writer must be relevant to the society, whose virtues and ideals he or she extols.

History has been a prime factor in the African experience. This inevitably results in the writers addressing the historical circumstances of the continent. The chapter on self, myth and historical consciousness examines this issue.

Time and place condition the writer's experience; hence the repetition of the saying that the writer is not an air plant. Two essays, written from a personal experience, examine the phenomenon of the writer's place in his or her writing. In the two essays, "Nativity and the Creative Process: The Niger Delta in my Poetry" and "Inviting the World Into the House of Words: The Writer, His Place, People and Audience," I use my own Niger Delta background to show the influence of landscape, folklore, and others to show the writer's rootedness to a specific place.

One essay uses Nigeria as an example to look ahead at what the literature of Africa would be and bring in the new millennium. The projections for the future are based on past and current happenings. Also there is the admission that an accident or a genius could establish a direction for national literature – one person blazes the trail and others follow.

The justification of African literature in the American literature curriculum draws attention to the relationship between modern African literature and African-American literature. The specific essay distinguishes African literature while also showing how indebted to it African-American literature is. The qualities of African literature help to broaden and deepen the conventional concepts of literature in the West.

The essays espouse a role for the writer in society, informed by the African indigenous traditions of literature. The book, thus, aptly begins with the challenges of the African writer today. The African writer, working in the tradition of his or her forebears in the oral tradition, is much aware of certain responsibilities to the society that nurtured him or her. The artist uses his or her talent to promote the positive values of the society. This rather didactic role seems to be a common attribute of most African writers, who decry corruption and other negative practices around. The writer fashions a vision for the elevation of the society and writes with the aim of making the society better than he or she met it. There appears to be a sense of urgency in the works of many

African writers because of the so many problems associated with underdevelopment and Third World that inhibit or hold back the humanity of the people. The writer's place and time are relevant in the fashioning of a personal role. The chapters on nativity, myth and historical consciousness and their impact on the writer reinforce the role of the writer in projecting his or her people's cultural identity.

The role of the African writer has been expanded to encompass more than the indigenous to reflect the current reality of the African. Africa has gone through various external and internal dynamics that have reshaped the culture into a new identity. The essays arise from the need, after so much has happened to Africa, to (re)order the fractured psyche into a wholesome imagination. The role of the African writer, at the forefront of the opening and concluding chapters, places the African writer beside writers from other cultures and continents and accentuates the special place writers find themselves in because of the continent's history, society, politics, and socio-economic conditions.

Literature matters from the African experience. Writers, for writing their minds on national issues, have been jailed and executed by military and civilian dictators in Africa. If they were not afraid of the power of the word, the nervousness of dictators in nations of vigorous writing would not be there. Literature has been in the vanguard of the liberation of modern Africa as seen in works against colonialism, economic mismanagement, political corruption, apartheid, and other negative factors that have plagued parts of the continent. Literature remains a vibrant form of opposition against the excesses of political leaders almost in every African country. It also draws attention to society's excesses and aims at sensitizing the readers' minds towards a more humane society. One of the later chapters deals with what literature has done in Africa and the rest of the world in countering different forms of terror. The concluding chapters, except the last on recent African poetry reviews, are linked with the early ones, since the question of the writer's role is touched again – this time on how writers have used their literary talent and expertise to struggle not only for personal freedom but for the overall struggle against evil in society. Literature, in the African experience, ranges on the side of good against the forces of evil, as it does on the side of the masses and the disadvantaged against dictators and exploiters.

It is my belief that these essays will be useful reading for writers, literary scholars, critics, and students of modern African literature and comparative literature, and the general reader of literature in contextualizing the African literary experience and imagination.

Charlotte, NC. August 3, 2005

Contents

Preface

1.	The challenges of the African writer today	1
2.	African culture and the New World Order	7
3.	Nativity and the creative process: The Niger Delta in my poetry	23
4.	African culture today	41
5.	Divine mentoring in poetry and its performance	57
6.	Self, myth and historical consciousness: an African writer's reflection	73
7.	Nigerian literature in the 21st century: what direction?	82
8.	Whose English?: The African writer and the language issue	92
9.	Expanding the curriculum in American schools: Why include African literature?	103
10.	How the Urhobo people see the world through art	112
11.	Countering terror in the literary world: the example of activism	121
12.	Anxieties and hopes: recent African poetry	135
13.	Inviting the world into the house of words: the writer, his place, people and audience	146
14.	Reviews of some published African poetry books	152

Index 163

I

The challenges of the African writer today*

A writer is not an air plant but the product of a specific place and time, which have their cultural, social, economic and political manifestations. Thus, he or she is intricately bound to the destiny of the place and time, which have nurtured him or her. The problems of the writer's place or environment and period are therefore the writer's own problems too. That is why the challenges of the writer in Africa today are, to a large extent, the challenges of his or her own African peoples arising from their being Africans in this era and by virtue of their environment.

These challenges also relate to the writer's tradition, which he or she has to adopt in an individual manner for self-expression. Challenges are based on the problems of the present and past experiences as well as a vision of the future. Thus Africa's past, present and future are important in the writer's fashioning of a vision. Is there nostalgia for the past from which certain values should be reclaimed? Is the present, compared to the past, deficient of expectations? What is the hope for the future? These are all relevant questions that need to be addressed by the concerned African writer of today. The challenges, therefore, relate to the writer's role in society and his or her relation to the African tradition of literature.

Art in traditional Africa has always been very utilitarian and the African writer of today cannot discard outright that tradition and just embrace art for art's sake. He or she has to be very mindful of the tradition, which can be interrogated, followed, or discarded. To be relevant to the experiences of his or her people, the writer has to start

---

* April 11, 1997, Originally published in *The Guardian* (Nigerian), Lagos.

from the tradition, which a special talent can broaden and deepen. This is especially important as Africa is currently facing a lot of pressing political, economic, social, and other problems. A certain measure of urgency has to inform the writer's voice to reflect the desperate times. Unlike most American or western writers and critics who consider political and economic issues to be extra-literary, the African literary artist has to address the political, socio-economic, and other realities of contemporary Africa.

In much of Africa there are serious political and economic problems. In mainly military regimes but also in civilian-ruled countries, there is disintegration of the democratic process. Military dictatorship is there to annul the will of the majority of people as in Nigeria and Algeria. The ruling elite is so corrupt that the country's wealth is carted away into personal accounts abroad, leaving the people in untold misery as in Nigeria and Congo DR. In many countries, there is political repression and no form of dissent is tolerated. Many writers have been harassed or thrown into jail as Wole Soyinka, Ngugi wa Thiongo, and Jack Mapanje, among others, have experienced. Worse still, a Nigerian writer, Ken Saro-Wiwa, was hanged for crying foul over the exploitation of his minority people and the degradation of the Niger Delta environment. Writers in Africa have been in the vanguard in the struggle for democracy and justice in their own and sometimes other countries. In this pursuit many face threats to their lives.

How do writers respond to the political challenges? Writers have become ever more political than at any time in African history. Writers use their medium to condemn tyranny, military dictatorship, oppression, and denial and violation of fundamental human rights.

Writers adopt different strategies. Today's Africa is comparable to Stalinist Russia, in which dissenting writers like Osip Mandelstam were sent to labour camps where they died. Mandelstam was sent to the labour camp ostensibly for referring to Stalin as the "Kremlin charioteer." As in the Stalinist era, many writers attempt to be subtle, self-censoring themselves by being as indirect as possible. I have personally done this in my "Fate of Vultures," in which fictional names echo real names of politicians so as to avoid libel and persecution. "Shamgari," "Shankari," and "Alexius" though fictional will remind anyone familiar with the Nigerian political landscape then of the president and his vice-president respectively.

Some writers are blunt, face threats to their lives, and run abroad, especially to the West. Ngugi wa Thiongo, Frank Chipasula, Jack

Mapanje, and Wole Soyinka are examples. Others become activists at home and risk jail or death – Ken Saro-Wiwa was hanged for his activist role on behalf of the Ogoni people of the Niger Delta. Wole Soyinka had to literally run through the forest to escape possible arrest or liquidation by the Sani Abacha operatives. The writer everywhere in Africa, as long as there are political problems, will increasingly be the moral guardian of his or her people's conscience.

A big challenge for the African writer today is to avoid reinforcing Western stereotypical notions of Africa in the exposure of Africa's frailties. It is true, as Chinua Achebe tells Bill Moyers, that the greed of African leaders goes beyond any human understanding. However, I believe the African writer today should, while criticizing Africa's socio-political problems, propose a vision of hope beyond current problems.

Similarly, African writers respond to the socio-economic plight of their people. The corrupt political leadership with its bureaucracy steals the national wealth, leaving the people in dire poverty. In many countries, there are not enough good roads, hospitals, and schools to meet the social and other basic needs of the people. The socio-economic challenge is very strong in Africa.

Writers have usually ranged on the side of the poor, the have-nots, and the underprivileged in their writings. From the mid-1970s till now, most writers appear to be to the left in their sympathy for the common people. In doing this, they criticize the corrupt leadership and indirectly ask for the bridging of the gap between the rich and the poor. Many writers, in their works, call for socio-economic justice. The exposure of corruption often irks the leadership and could lead to the persecution of the writer.

Thus, the African writer faces risks in political and economic spheres. There is a lot of pressure on writers at home. There is the temptation to shut one's eyes to the urgent problems at home for one's safety and write literature without any attention to what is around. This will please the "emperor," as Chinua Achebe would put it. Those forced out for political, economic, and personal reasons tend to adjust to other traditions abroad. Every writer has a choice, but there should be no prostitution or pandering to other traditions in an attempt to gain sympathy from others, especially in the West.

The economic challenge affects the writer in the publishing side. In Africa most of the journals such as *Okike* and *Black Orpheus* have, for years, stopped publication. Likewise the publishing houses have either stopped or scaled down their publication of creative works. Heinemann and Longman that used to publish many African literary works have either drastically reduced their publication to reprints of old popular texts and a few novels or totally stopped. There has been no single collection of poems by an African author published by Heinemann for so many years. In Nigeria only Malthouse Press, Heinemann (Nigeria), and Spectrum publish creative writings; in Ghana it is only Woeli. Also active are Baobab Press in Zimbabwe, East African Publishing House in Kenya, and a host of presses in South Africa. Because of its relative strong economy, South Africa has the most publishing houses in Africa today – many of the international publishers are still there. Thus, there are few or no publishing avenues at home for most African writers, especially the young ones. This is a serious challenge to creativity in Africa.

Many writers pay to publish as is done with Nigeria's Kraft Books based at Ibadan, which asks for subsidies from many writers. Some writers publish themselves outright and this has serious consequences of not going through channels of editors who might help to improve the text and the quality of the book production. Others whether at home or abroad write to publish abroad. Western agents and editors want either what is quaintly interesting or what their European or North American readers are familiar with. Publishing, they are quick to remind one, is a business and not a philanthropic work. Thus, they select some kinds of books from Africa. It is interesting that Ben Okri is now considered (and considers himself) a British writer!

Publishing abroad involves many compromises on the side of the African writer. If, for instance, the writer is publishing in the United States, the African manuscript will be edited to fit not only American spelling, punctuation, and grammatical style but also African words are deliberately changed into American equivalents for the readership. The African reader of works of Nurrudin Farah's *Secrets* as well as of other American editions of African literary works will shake his head at what is being sacrificed for American comprehension! Younger African writers abroad go as far as writing with a foreign Western audience in mind. It takes an experienced African writer to balance his truthfulness to his people and tradition with western commercial concerns.

There are strong challenges for the African writer today. Not many people read, and many of the young ones who read buy Western romance novels. How does the African writer meet this challenge? African writers have to diversify their themes and form so as to convey experiences with which readers can identify. Also to meet the challenge of readers who may not be highly educated, writers may have to work out ways of writing not only in Standard English but also in their own languages, any African lingua franca, or Pidgin English. If writers go back to their indigenous traditions, they should come out with forms and techniques that will enhance the understanding of their works. The writer has to continuously explore avenues of reflecting not only the experiences of the people but the language patterns, even if these have to be anglicized. This specific challenge has to do with the African writer of today and his or her readership.

There are some challenges from outside that need to be mentioned. There is a gradual westernizing of the globe. One is given the European/American model as the best or the touchstone by which everything else is judged. African writers are not to clone or imitate Western writers whose literary traditions at the moment seem to have lost steam. Rather, they should experiment from the wealth of their oratures. Literature should be in the vanguard of Africa's cultural preservation. By this, I do not mean it should just be a relic of the past but should be a means to re-fashion a dynamic culture. In this pursuit, literature should be used to question cultural values, which could lead to some foreign ones being absorbed and some indigenous ones being discarded. If there is any attempt by one culture to assimilate Africans, literature should be the last stand in the culture war.

A closely related challenge to African writers today is the resurgence of neo-modernist criticism of African literature. Since the criticism and publishing of African creative works are coming from the West, there has been in recent years a spate of western critics and their African cohorts who, as in the early 1960s, use western critical standards to judge African texts. There are many instances of this, including Stewart Brown's comments on contemporary Nigerian poetry, which involves my own poetry. However, I will give one other example. Harold A. Waters, in his review of *New Poets of West Africa* edited by Tijan M. Sallah, writes that "...*New Poets* is a *bad* anthology *from the viewpoint of Western aesthetics*" (emphasis mine) [*World Literature Today*, 70/3, Summer 1996, 746]. In that vein, every good Western literary work could be *bad from the viewpoint of African aesthetics*! African writers, who are not mature and strong enough, could be pressured or misled to adopt a strange aesthetic. At the bottom of it, literature is a cultural production; hence its aesthetics are also cultural. I want to answer the likes of Waters as Sharon Dolin has done of the criticism of free verse by formalists and language poets. To Dolin, "Standards need to be based on how successful a given poem is within a certain aesthetic – not on how much it fails within another" (*AWP Chronicle*, 9/3 [December 1996], 13).

The writer in Africa today has to take risks and be very courageous. There should be a stronger commitment, persistence, patience, and faith for a positive vision. Whatever is good will some day get published. Are we ready to sacrifice so much for the muse and deny ourselves so much? The older writers have to encourage the younger ones to keep on and expand the tradition.

Furthermore, the writer in Africa today is to give hope to his or her people. After all, once hope is lost, everything else is lost. Things may be so bad politically and economically in much of Africa today, but one should not lose hope. The writer should continue the subtle didacticism – while reflecting life, he or she should give voice to the voiceless, the underprivileged, poor, women, disabled, and others of the underclass. Dictators, oppressors, and exploiters will continue to see writers as threats to their negative ways. As Chinua Achebe puts it in *Anthills of the Savannah* (141), "storytellers are a threat. They threaten all champions of control; they frighten usurpers of the right-to-freedom of the human spirit – in state, in church or mosque, in party congress, in the university or wherever."

Thus, the challenges from society, culture, and politics are many. There are internal and external challenges. There are challenges from the New World Order, which could swamp Africa with alien practices and values. There are also challenges in the content, form, and vision expressed in African creative writings today. But the writer has to take risks, adjust to peculiarities, and be courageous. While they continue to wrestle with challenges, writers should owe responsibility to their people and art. They should not give prescriptions, but, in Achebe's words again, "give headaches" (148) to all negative forces in the continent.

II

African culture and the new world order*

On the surface, a world without opposing ideological blocs is a welcome development as the threat of a global military confrontation is drastically diminished. The collapse of the old Soviet Union in 1988 gave rise to the 'new world order'. While this New World Order is often discussed in relation to politics, trade, economics, democracy, human rights, and communication, no attention has been paid to its impact on non-western cultures. Africa has been marginalized because of its inability to compete globally in modern technology. While the New World Order talks of global economy, global information networks, and other global standards, it is mainly a creation of the Atlantic Powers headed by the United States. These European world countries will use the New World Order to promote their interests and cultural values worldwide at the expense of Africa. It is in the area of culture that Africa is likely to suffer the most damage. I intend, therefore, to discuss the possible impact of the New World Order on African culture based on prevailing trends in the European world countries and contemporary Africa.

African culture has always been dynamic and responsive to internal and external pressures; hence African culture is often described in terms of being traditional, modern, and contemporary. In other words, African culture is not static; hence new and recent developments in

---

* Written in 1995 for a collection of essays on Africa and the New World Order that Luis Serapiao of Howard University, Washington, DC, was trying to put together. The same essay was later presented to the Summer Institute organized by Dr. Frank Eguaroje at The University of North Carolina at Greensboro.

world history such as the New World Order are bound to affect its dynamics.

Traditional African culture involves the way of life before Europeans came to Africa. Many anthropologists have portrayed this way of life as if it was a static and unchanging mosaic of habits. Works of Melville Herskovits among the Fon of present-day Benin Republic and Albert Schweitzer in the Ogoue area of Gabon could be seen in the light of a pristine and unpolluted African culture.[1] In traditional African culture, humans have been able to relate to and bend the natural environment for their survival. Farming, fishing, and hunting were practiced to produce food for man's basic sustenance. Animals were not hunted for commercial purposes, unless to barter for other basic needs at a local level. At the same time, men married women to procreate to have children to help them in their occupations and to keep on the family or group name. The traditional culture was identified with the "primitive" and what appeared exotic to the Westerner. In fairness, some of these anthropologists dealt seriously with the philosophy of life of different African groups as P. Tempels with groups in the Congo.[2]

Many African artists might have reinforced this purist view by creating an idyllic and Edenic picture of a tranquil ancient Africa. Such Negritude writers as Leopold Sedar Senghor and Birago Diop portray ancient Africa in very sensuous imagery as a haven of nature, happiness, dancing and singing. In this imagined golden age of Africa, there is harmony of the human, natural and cosmic in a romantic setting. This depiction has contributed to the image of a static traditional African culture.

At the extreme side, and exaggerated to counter the golden age view, is Yambo Ouologuem's *Bound to Violence*, which created all sorts of violence imaginable to characterize traditional Africa, which was depicted as savage and barbaric. This reactive view also destroyed the image of the noble savage in the undisturbed primeval African cultural setting. This might have informed many European writings about Africa in pre-colonial and colonial times and Joseph Conrad's *Heart of Darkness* set in present-day Congo Democratic Republic and Joyce Cary's *Mister Johnson* set in Nigeria fall into this category of a

---

[1] Melville Herskovits's findings on the Fon are published in *Dahomey, vols. I & II*, New York: J.J. Augustin, 1938. Albert Schweitzer's experience is expressed in his *African Notebook*. New York: H. Holt, 1939.
[2] P. Tempels's work on Bantu philosophy.

barbaric African culture. Of course, the creator of Tarzan who never set foot on Africa belongs to this class that viewed African culture as barbaric.

Somewhere in-between the golden age and the violent schools of African culture is Chinua Achebe's portrayal in *Things Fall Apart* of the Igbo society before the coming of Europeans. It is a way of life, which had its strengths and weaknesses but was changing. It was communal, democratic, spiritual, and very well organized. In short, it was a self-reliant culture. According to Achebe,

> African people did not hear of culture for the first time from Europeans...their societies were not mindless but frequently had a philosophy of great depth and value and beauty...they had poetry and, above all, they had dignity.[3]

In Achebe's portrayal of traditional culture, changes were taking place including the reduction of punishment for certain crimes such as the violation of the Week of Peace or inadvertent murder. In earlier times any person who violated the Week of Peace was dragged on the ground until the person died. This was abandoned because the harsh punishment itself ran counter to the peace the period was meant to promote. In place of what was apparently a death sentence, a fine was now meted on the violator. This was the practice in the Igbo area between about 1870 and 1910, the approximate period of the historical setting of *Things Fall Apart*. Similarly, the punishment for inadvertent murder had become milder. Instead of exile for life, there was now only a seven-year exile of atonement. Even within the culture there were liberals and conservatives like Obierika and Okonkwo respectively. While the liberals wanted changes, the conservatives, represented by Okonkwo, wanted to stick rigidly to old values. There were arguments in the traditional society about certain practices such as the throwing away of twins and one can infer from earlier changes that, even without the coming of European missionaries and colonialists, the likes of Obierika and Nwoye would have with time been able to effect changes from within. In this way of life, therefore, there are changes, but these changes take a long time to come by.

---

[3] Quoted in G.D. Killam (ed.) *African Writers on African Writing*, London: Heinemann, 1973, p.8

This traditional way of life still persists in mainly rural areas in many parts of Africa today. The communal, democratic, and spiritual life still imbues traditional African society with many of the mores and values that sustained African forefathers. Families are still closely knit and each member still defends its name by living a worthy life. It is this type of society in the Old Oyo Kingdom in which the family of the Elesin Oba (the King's Horseman) strangled him if he refused to ritually end his life and be buried with the late Alafin. This was done for the family's honour. In Wole Soyinka's *Death and the King's Horseman*, Olunde (the Horseman's senior son) had to perform his father's duty when the Elesin Oba failed to kill himself at the appropriate time, as custom demanded. It did not matter whether it was Elesin Oba's personal weakness or the intervention by the white man. The ritual had to be done, and Olunde did it to save the family's name and honour.

The spiritual life with its many sects and service of spiritual mentors and healers like the medicine-man and diviner is still vibrant. John S. Mbiti puts it succinctly: "Wherever the African is, there is his religion."[4] Many Africans tend to hold to many traditional ways despite their living in cities or in foreign countries in contemporary times.

African culture after the colonization of Africa by European countries could not remain traditional. Modern African culture, therefore, is postcolonial in a sense; it is the result of the epoch-making encounter between Africa and Europe for better or for worse. Africa has been opened to the rest of the world and has been both a centrifugal and focal point in world happenings. Thus, qualities which writers like John Mbiti in *African Religions and Philosophy* and Mazisi Kunene in *The Ancestors and the Sacred Mountain* have used to endow Africa have been so exposed as to be at times in conflict with modern historical developments.

Unlike before the coming of Europeans, changes in the postcolonial period have come at a faster and multitudinous rate and make Africans sometimes confused as to what the African way of life really is. Poets such as Gabriel Okara of Nigeria and Okot p'Bitek of Uganda have portrayed the ensuing conflict in their respective *The Fisherman's Invocation* and *Song of Lawino*. Okara sees a culture conflict in the modern African faced with both traditional African ways and the new European ways represented by the drum and the piano respectively.

---

[4] John S. Mbiti, *African Religions and Philosophy*, Oxford: Heinemann, 1989, p.2.

The new music is thus dissonant in its being neither pure African nor European, a situation that leaves the poet wondering about his identity. But that was the "morning mist" of a new age, a period of transition, and one can understand the confused state of things.

Similarly, Okot p'Bitek presents African and European ways; the African in a favourable light and the European in a negative light, through opposing images. Africans are presented as dignified and beautiful like the bull and the giraffe, while the Europeans are compared to the monkey and chicken. Lawino represents the authentic African naturally endowed with vitality, artistic versatility, and morality. Ocol and Clementine are the Africans who copy European ways without consideration for their relevance in the African environment and so look ridiculous in the African setting.

This contest between African and European ways continued to obsess many African writers. By the time Wole Soyinka wrote *The Lion and the Jewel*, the Nigerian dramatist appeared to promote the tried and stable African ways of life at the expense of the untried European, which were out of place. This explains the dramatist's negative portrayal of Lakunle, the schoolteacher and promoter of European values. He is presented as ridiculous in his dressing, superficial in his understanding of Western ways, and very ineffectual as a young man. On the other side is Baroka, the traditional chief who in spite of his age is full of vitality, experienced, and absorptive of new ways that he feels will strengthen him. Baroka is deeply rooted and evinces self-confidence and wins the "jewel," Sidi, who becomes his new wife. Soyinka and P'Bitek emphasize that only what is relevant needs to be borrowed from outside. But that period of transition in Africa is long gone.

African culture has been made more complex by the appearance of Islam in the continent. Though Islam reached some parts of Africa before Christianity, it has for long been identified with mainly Arab North Africa. But Islam has spread beyond North Africa to the savannah areas of West Africa and parts of East Africa such as Zanzibar (Tanzania) and the Mombasa area of Kenya. Islam is not just a religion but a way of life, and this further compounds the indigenous culture of Islamized parts of sub-Saharan Africa. Because Muslims formed the ruling class in many areas they conquered at the beginning of the nineteenth century, there was a certain discord between the indigenes who though Muslims wanted to remain with their native culture and the aristocrats who followed strict Islamic dictates. Thus, among the Mossi, while the political power lay with the Islamic aristocrats, the spiritual power lay with indigenous priests who served the native gods. In much of northern Nigeria, Islam has almost succeeded in wiping out the indigenous traditional culture. It is no surprise that in these areas very little traditional art survives beyond crafts, since Islam forbids the sculpturing of human and animal figures which is a dominant art form of traditional Africa.

What Ali Mazrui has described as the "triple heritage"[5] of Africa has thus for many decades been deeply entrenched. Traditional African, Islamic, and European values make modern African culture. Thus, Africa has for long not been its pristine self that anthropologists would make us believe it is. Rather, forces of history have impressed upon it a multifaceted identity, which still survives and is so deeply ingrained that the hybridity cannot be shed without losing some aspects of modern African culture.

African culture has imbibed what it needed from outside while retaining its authenticity. It is difficult for a free people to control their varying responses to foreign ways of life. One aspect of the New World Order, which does not bode well for Africa, is modern technology. As Kunene has stated in *The Ancestors and the Sacred Mountain*, Africa is developed ethically, unlike the European world, which has developed technologically. Thus, "where other societies describe social and material progress in identical terms of growth from lower levels to higher levels, African society separates the two, depicting the ethical element and the technological aspects as often capable of moving in opposing directions."[6] Kunene affirms the African viewpoint that "a highly ethically advanced society need not necessarily be technologically advanced; equally a technologically advanced society does not automatically possess a high ethical level."[7]

Currently Africans seem to be mesmerized by sophisticated technological gadgets such as stereo, cars, televisions, and mobile phones. Today it is not surprising to have cable television with CNN and MTV in rural Africa. Unlike countries such as Iran and China which are rightly worried about the influx of American and Western ideas, African states do not seem to protect themselves against this technological onslaught. At one time it might have been good to be

---

[5] Ali Mazrui in *The Africans: a triple heritage*, Boston: Little, Brown, 1986.
[6] Mazisi Kunene, *The Ancestors and the Sacred Mountain*, London: Heinemann, 1982, p. xi.
[7] Ibid., p.xi.

exposed to European education and other ways, but now uncontrolled exposure threatens the very fabric of African cultural identity.

The New World Order was proclaimed after the collapse of the old Soviet Union, which virtually emasculated the Eastern Bloc and left only the western Bloc now generally described as the western Alliance. When the Old World Order had two opposing rival ideological blocs, Africa was like a bride – wooed by each bloc. While the ideological contest for Africa's heart could be destabilizing politically, as was the case in Angola, Ethiopia, and Somalia among others, it left African culture to be respected by either bloc. Whether this respect was genuine or not did not matter, but neither side in the Cold War days could afford to antagonize Africans as a race without reaping its adverse political consequences. Generally speaking, African nationalists felt the East was more sympathetic to Africa's problems in the Cold War period. Many liberation movements in Africa received moral, financial, and military support from the former Soviet Union and China. Before the late 1980s, it was anathema and politically incorrect in Africa for any but the corrupt to openly identify with the West. The likes of Mobutu Sese Seko, Houphuet-Boigny, and Kamuzu Banda, who were close to the West, were seen more as reactionaries. Most politicians and artists ranged on the side of the common people and openly proclaimed themselves socialists. Ngugi wa Thiongo, the Kenyan writer, and Festus Iyayi of Nigeria were some of the most ideological at the time. In a brief spelloff self-rehabilitation and in order to restore his sagging popularity in Zaire and Africa, Mobutu announced the policy of "authenticity" in which he changed the former Congo (Leopoldville) to Zaire, asked Zaireans to have African indigenous names, wear African clothes, and popularized the leopard colours of Zairean attire. For a brief period he was seen as a nationalist before he further went to plunder Zaire's natural resources.

The New World Order, which focuses on globalization of political and economic systems, is a euphemism for European world-approved values rather than African or Asian. The New World Order therefore has been brought about by the Western Alliance and promotes American and European interests and values. It benefits mainly its promoters, the technologically advanced, the rich, and the militarily powerful. The United States of America, the only superpower now on earth, and her West European allies have the wherewithal economically, militarily, and thus politically to force African countries to uphold what she considers to be "civilized" values or conduct. In issues such as female circumcision and family planning, the American norm automatically becomes the universal standard. Africa without economic, military and political power cannot compete favourably in the New World cultures. One of the major complaints by African and Third World women at the Fourth World Conference on Women in Beijing has been that the rich countries use their wealth to promote their western values in the name of being progressive on women's issues. In fact, African women felt that western feminists were pushing their ideas of so-called "sexual rights" on the rest of the world. Somehow, American and the European Union women were very aggressive over issues such as lesbianism and other "sexual rights" that African, Arab and Catholic Latin American women felt were not central to the woman's condition at the end of the twentieth century.

Some major issues that the New World Order addresses are trade, human rights, democratization, communication, and transportation. These issues benefit the technologically advanced, and Africa is not yet in that high league. But what is important is the multifarious ways these issues will deluge Africa with alien values, swamp its nativity, and wipe out indigenous values and ways.

The New World Order calls for trade liberalization to open world markets for competition. Africa was the lone loser in the just-concluded GATT talks as the North American, European and Asian groups defended their respective turf. African countries are overwhelmingly importers of western products ranging from cars to textiles and foods. In fact, the few industries in most African countries have been starved of raw materials because of their impoverished economies, which they generally attribute to harsh recommendations of the World Bank and the International Monetary Fund, major western economic institutions. Of the Group of Seven that meets secretly to direct world economies, none of the members is African!

What has the trade dimension of the New World Order got to do with African culture? It has so much to do with it. Since Africans are chronic importers of manufactured products from the European world countries, their lifestyle is conditioned by outside tastes. The car, dress, food, and other luxuries are derived from the West. Even the traditional African dresses are sewn with fabrics manufactured in the West. West African men and women might have a flair for flowing gowns, but the lace, jacquard, and brocade materials used to sew the African dresses are imported from Europe. Groups such as the Igbo, Ijo, and Urhobo of Nigeria see their imported hats as traditional attire! The "wrappers" used in many sub-Saharan societies are manufactured in Birmingham, UK, Holland or France! With the liberalization of trade, the rich western countries will have uncontrolled access to African markets and the alien modes will eventually become African staple. Africa might also sell some of its dresses abroad but that will mainly be to Black groups in the Americas and Europe, a market that pales before the huge exports of Europe and North America.

Another favourite of the New World Order is democratization or political pluralism. Many Africans tend to swallow wholesale western ideas of government and consequently fail to conduct research into their own indigenous political systems. This position is understandable when one bears in mind the many autocratic rulers and military juntas in Africa. But borrowing the United States' presidential model or the British parliamentary model, or the French presidential model is like transplanting a tundra-flourishing plant into the tropical zone. The chances of its growing and surviving are extremely slim. But whatever the theoretical merit of modernizing African traditional institutions or indigenizing foreign models, the trend today is for Africa to try the electoral experience of the European world countries with a view to finding a solution to its seemingly endemic political instability.

A major casualty of the borrowed electoral system is the communal life that characterizes traditional African culture. The voting system promotes radical individualism, which in the lust for power ignores integrity to lure voters. The open ballot system started in Kenya and successfully used in Nigeria in the early 1990s calls for voters to line up behind their candidates to be counted publicly. The merit of this is that there is no room for mischief as in the secret ballot in which boxes could be stuffed full before voting started. However, this open ballot system is often decried in Eurocentric circles as coercive. Opponents of the open ballot seem to ignore the fact that the principles of democracy "may prevail in a wide variety of political arrangements and practices, which naturally vary according to historical conditions."[8] Claude Ake adds that "Traditional African political systems were infused with democratic values...everything was everybody's business, engendering a strong emphasis on participation. Standards of accountability were even stricter than in western societies."[9]

---

[8] Claude Ake, "Rethinking African Democracy," *Journal of Democracy*, vol. 2, no. 1 (Winter 1991), p. 34.
[9] Ibid., p. 34.

The new multi-party system tends to place premium on wealth as a source of political power. In most African countries practicing western-type democracies, it will be almost impossible for a politician who is not rich to become President. Political power is for sale and millionaires are the power brokers and grabbers. This could corrupt an ethically advanced people and make them to be rogues in office.

In addition, the democratic by-product of the New World Order will greatly reduce the influence of traditional rulers who are custodians of African culture. Chieftaincy with its paraphernalia is a cultural treasure. African chieftaincy institutions are eroded by western-style democracies since individuals no longer feel very obliged to their communities and groups. The Ashanti, BaKongo, Bamileke, Benin, and Ife kingdoms, among others, would not have produced their classical art without the royal institutions.

The New World Order also promotes global communication and transportation. The major satellites in orbit are western-owned. With cable television being sold to the most rural of places in Africa without any control, Africa has been inundated with foreign radio and television programs that reflect the worldview of their western producers. The cases of CNN and MTV, both American, tell this western cultural domination. CNN is not just a news network but a propagator of American lifestyles and values. It exposes American fashion and habits, which in many cases run counter to African cultural ideals. A case in point is the use of guns and love of violence in American screens. The wielding of guns and the glamorization of violence in newscasts could influence a people who look to the United States for fashionable trends. Africans dress in a dignified way but the western cultural practice of overexposure of the body with mini-dresses could gain currency in African urban areas. The influence of American violence on Africa is already prevalent in the armed robberies in different parts of Africa. The same negative influence could come from the widespread use of drugs in America, as African youths could be deceived to think it is the trendy thing to do. Thus, in the areas of lifestyles signalled by American dress codes, violence, sex-prone movies, and drug use, African culture could be adversely affected as the New World Order progresses. African youths are especially vulnerable, as they do not seem to see much creativity or cultural vitality currently in Africa and, in the absence of this, they imitate the alien trends. The European world-led New World Order could propel African cultural nationalists to be creative of new ways to counter the alien ones.

Africa cannot promote its own culture effectively before the onslaught of American and European cable networks. The materialism of the West is so glamorized that African youths will be hooked to a consumerism that will adversely affect the spiritual dimension of their African background. The African may be poor but is spiritually rich. Since the New World Order through its global information networks will break down barriers to the flow of information in African societies, western and western-style advertising will sway many Africans to become like many Americans – compulsive consumers. That could lead the youths to abandon the simple life of their parents and go for money at all cost to afford the new luxuries. As mentioned earlier, the drug culture of the West could be sold to unknowing Africans as a fashionable lifestyle. The highly secularized western societies would adversely affect African culture in the crosscurrents of today's communication.

Language is a major vehicle of culture. African languages could suffer immensely from the New World Order. In the effort to be current, European languages like English and French will be promoted at the expense of African languages. With world trade, world communication, and world diplomacy, the foreign languages will so preoccupy Africa as to leave no space for the development of indigenous languages. However, the industrialized western countries have started to study African languages for trade and diplomatic reasons with the understanding that to deal with a people effectively one needs to know their culture. A programme like the American Department of Defence's National Security Education Program (NSEP), which focuses on language and area studies, is geared towards competing effectively in the New World Order.

African social roles are threatened by the New World Order. One of the major aspects of African culture is the respect for elders. Increasing individualism promoted by the West could influence children not to respect their elders as in the United States, where a ten-year old calls his fifty-five-year old teacher by his first name. Children are driven from home to fend for themselves because they have reached the age of eighteen. While the westerner might argue that this would teach the teenager the importance of responsibility, the African prefers a close-knit family. The African family could forsake its extended nature to be nuclear as the western family. The communal values could be shed for a self-centred individualism, in which "me" counts more than "us."

Other cultural practices of the West, hawked as civilized behaviour, could become rampant in Africa. For instance, there is a general uproar against child labour in the West. In Africa children, especially after school, help in farm work and trade. The income they earn helps to supplement whatever the family earns for its sustenance. This though is different from depriving children from going to school and exploiting them for purely profit motives. The way children should be treated could become contentious in Africa. The Fourth Women's Conference in Beijing again is a case in point. African women/parents like most of those from the Third World argued for parents' responsibilities to outweigh teenagers' rights to privacy. The European Union and American delegates argued for teenagers' rights of privacy at the expense of parents' responsibilities. In the end there was a compromise that the needs of both must be taken into account, but it shows how western ways could be pushed on the rest of the world.

On a positive note, human rights might be extended to include how the powerful countries treat the small ones, not just how non-western rulers treat their citizens. Issues such as repatriation of stolen art and money will be discussed. I foresee embarrassment of being accused of double standards prompting many powerful countries to redeem their image of hypocrisy. Germany and Poland are asking Russia to return the artworks stolen from them; Italy is asking Germany to return her looted artworks. There is so much of African art outside the continent and there are already calls for the repatriation of such works. In February 1995, a British parliamentarian has come on the side of Africans for the return of looted art and I understand that Britain is returning the Queen Idia headpiece, the symbol of Black and African world cultures in the 1977 art festival in Nigeria.

Similar requests for repatriation and reparation will be made. Africa is replete with corrupt leaders as in Zaire and Nigeria who steal money and bank abroad especially in Swiss banks. If Switzerland returned corrupt money to the Philippines, why should she not return the billions of dollars put in secret coded accounts by African leaders, more so when such money could make such a big difference in the lives of the common people? Already Swiss banks have set aside huge amounts to compensate Jewish survivors of the Holocaust. World opinion could build up against countries in Europe and North America that profited from the slave trade and still enrich their economies in other ways at the expense of poorer countries.

African patriarchies will be hard put to test on the roles of women as waves of western ideas influence their women to revolt against traditional roles. As the New World Order gains more currency in Africa, the battle for women's rights and equality will intensify and fracture African societies with dire consequences for the culture. Single-parent families could escalate in the gender war brought to Africa. There appears to be an inevitable weakening of the African family, which may gradually lose its cohesive nature. Practices like bride-wealth ceremonies in marriages are being questioned by Westerners who do not understand them and feel that African women are being sold in marriage. They do not understand the compensation for the parents' labour as the woman will from marriage become "one" with her man and separate from the parents who laboured to bring her up and spent so much money to educate her. The western dowry system in which the woman's parents pay for the marriage celebration is not seen as a bribe to the man! The divorce rate in otherwise stable marriages in Africa will increase as in the West where after a marriage it is a matter of when the divorce will take place. In fact, there is the joke in the United States as couples marry for the ETD (Estimated Time of Divorce).

African culture continues to change from identifiable material icons such as dress, music, dance, scarifications, and masks. The policies of the New World Order will further erase African cultural marks. Deep-rooted beliefs in spirituality, ideas about the cyclical nature of life, time and space, aesthetics, and other immaterial aspects of the culture will replace the visible. The extended family, as indicated earlier, could suffer from new trends that emphasize the individual and the self first. Informal education of young ones as parents do in the evenings will be abandoned as children get obsessed with western entertainment tools as the television, video player, and computer games. That will further weaken the children's grasp of experiences that can help them live fulfilling lives in their African environment. The New World Order will thus increase the influence of Euro-American culture, which will consequently undermine the indigenous African culture. African youths in particular will be alienated from their roots.

Africa is heading for a hybridity that literary theorists like Homi Bhabha see as an inevitable postcolonial trend.[10] African culture is moving from even that postcolonial hybridity to a near-swamping of its

---

[10] Mentioned in Bill Ashcroft *et alia*, *The Empire Writes Back*, New York: Routledge, 1989.

ways by the European culture whose technology is able to impose its values and codes on others without any military expeditions. African culture will be further bastardized, as its true nature will be difficult to determine.

The future of African culture in the New World Order depends on many factors beyond its control. Since the Order itself is still very new, its terms and impact cannot yet be fully told. Already there are hints of disaffection with technology even as it excites most Westerners. The intrusion of people's privacy, environmental pollution, technologically enhanced crimes, and an increasingly conservative political climate in the European world countries could cause mistrust of technology. Already there is a growing realization that western culture by its promotion of technology is self-destructive. The cars emit fumes; the factories emit carcinogenic chemicals which destroy the earth's ozone layer. The scientists never stop to think whether they really need something before making it once they know how to. Already too they are playing with genes and cloning and nobody knows where this will lead humanity.

In any case, there is a declining interest in some of the major vehicles of western popular culture. The ratings of MTV have plummeted in the United States and this could make it reassess its philosophy. The Internet, which has made many Americans to label the next century the "computer century," is increasingly being misused and bound to provoke a debate as to the necessity of travelling in cyberspace or the electronic super-highway. Discontent with technology in the West may affect its deployment to Africa and may save the culture further erosion. But from experience the West may discard something at home and still promote it in overseas markets. For instance, while asbestos has been banned in the United States since the 1970s, some American companies still build asbestos-producing factories all over Africa. The same can be said of cigarettes. While cigarette consumption is declining in the United States because it is scientifically proven to be a health hazard, American tobacco manufacturers have been exporting more overseas. Thus, the discontent with technology as it now is may not help to slow down the influence the West may have on African culture.

Many culture theorists might speak of evolution from a non-literate and oral state to a literate state, from primitivism to modernity. The place of what Walter Ong calls "secondary orality"[11] in modern culture is very important as radio, television, video, and film are in the vanguard of acculturation.

At the same time cultures like civilizations fluctuate. A culture could be vibrant at some periods of history and at others may be decadent. Thus, there is a cyclic movement of cultures that could rise to a certain apogee and later collapse into decadence. African culture in the New World Order is a long way from the African culture that Placide Tempels and Melville Herskovits experienced. New developments brought by the New World Order will open up the African continent to an influx of foreign ways that may swamp the continent's former cultural identity. I do not advocate what postmodernists will sarcastically describe as a return to primitivism or a pristine essentialist African state. But Africa is in a precarious position in the New World Order because of its poor economies and indiscriminate openness to the rest of the world.

Africa may never go to the extent of getting so assimilated into the western culture to the degree of accepting, among others, that the dog (rather than the Supreme God or man's neighbour) is man's best friend or the practice of two men or two women marrying each other. However, its culture will be highly threatened by foreign tastes and values that the New World Order promotes. With a superior technology, the West has everything to gain and African culture so much to lose in the new postcolonial dispensation euphemistically tagged the New World Order. In fact, one could term the New World Order as western cultural imperialism in a world in which the overt use of military force to subdue others to do your bidding has become embarrassingly crude. African cultural identity is already highly diluted. But as long as there are a people, they will have a culture and there is every hope that African culture will survive the New World Order which may just be a historical phase in the unending drama of human exploitation of the less advantaged.

---

[11] Secondary orality is discussed in Walter J. Ong's *Orality and Literacy: The Technologizing of the Word*, London/New York: Methuen, 1982.

References

Achebe, Chinua, *Things Fall Apart*. London: Heinemann, 1958.
Herskovits, Melville, *Dahomey*, vols. *I and II*, New York: J.J. Augustin, 1938.
Irele, Abiola. *The African Experience in Literature and Ideology*, London: Heinemann, 1981.
Jahn, Janheinz. *Muntu: an outline of the new African culture*, New York: Grove, 1961.
Killam, G.D. (ed.) *African Writers on African Writing*, London: Heinemann, 1973.
Kunene, Mazisi, *The Ancestors and the Sacred Mountain*, London: Heinemann, 1982.
Mazrui, Ali, *The Africans: a triple heritage*, Boston: Little, Brown, 1986.
Mbiti, John S., *African Religions and Philosophy*, Oxford: Heinemann, 1989.
Okara, Gabriel, *The Fisherman's Invocation*, Benin: Ethiope Press, 1978.
Ong, Walter J., *Orality and Literacy: The Technologizing of the Word*, London/New York: Methuen, 1982.
Ouologuem, Yambo, *Bound to Violence*, London: Heinemann, 1978.
P'Bitek, Okot, *Song of Lawino*, Nairobi: EAPH, 1965.
Schweitzer, Albert, *African Notebook*, New York: H. Holt, 1939.
Soyinka, Wole, *The Lion and the Jewel*, Oxford: OUP, 1965.
Tempels, P., *Bantu Philosophy*, Paris, 1959.

III

Nativity and the creative process: the Niger Delta in my poetry

As said elsewhere, the creative writer is never an air plant, but someone who is grounded in some specific place. It is difficult to talk of many writers without their identification with place. Every writer's roots are very important in understanding his or her work. For example, though born in Harlem to southern migrants in 1924, James Baldwin told an interviewer:

> I am, in all but in technical fact, a Southerner. My father was born in the South – my mother was born in the South, and if they had waited two more seconds I might have been born in the South. But that means I was raised by families whose roots were essentially southern rural (quoted in Hall 22).

Similarly, Zora Neale Hurston, wherever she lived, considered Eatonville, Florida, her home. As Cheryl A. Wall puts it, wherever Hurston journeyed, she "was able to draw on this heritage and find the strength to remain herself" (27). Claude McKay of Jamaican origin but living in Harlem wrote *A Long Way from Home*. Many African-Americans see Africa as their ancestral home. Even in the so-called mainstream American literature, William Faulkner's strength as a novelist comes from his Southern nativity. The writer's roots and heritage arise from his or her nativity.

Nativity has much to do with creating literature, especially poetry. The writer tends to exploit memory and return to childhood days to garner images to clarify his or her vision. I may have travelled extensively all over the world, I may have lived in different parts of Nigeria; I may be currently living and working in the United States, but my native home is the Niger Delta. Friends and readers of my writing say that I light up and become passionate when I write about the Niger Delta. Call that nostalgia, but I call it the immense power of the Niger Delta as my native place, the constant backdrop to my inspiration. In this reflection, I will use the Niger Delta in the context of my nativity to discuss the inexhaustible field of imagination that the writer draws from in the creative process.

Space is a major defining factor in African culture. Every African is in one way or another connected or linked to some specific place. In other words, space defines both the rootedness and heritage of people in Africa. That is why where one is born is important. It is a life-long badge one wears. I use nativity to mean birthplace and/or the place where one grows up to imbibe its worldview. Generally, where one is born or lives the formative years of childhood defines the person's nativity.

Nativity is some specific place, whose air, water, crops, folklore and other produce nourish the individual. This nourishment is not only physical but also spiritual. One can say that space in this context is geography. However, as Jose Ortega y Gasset hypothesizes, "Each geographic space, insofar as it is a space for a possible history, is ...a function of many variables" (quoted in Mudimbe 188). These "variables" include biology, economics, and language. Biologically, humans submit to the "demands of an environment, coming to terms with the modifications it imposes" (190). Michel Foucault sees humans as having needs and desires which they seek to satisfy economically. He also sees the human need for *meaning* resulting in arranging a *system* of signs (quoted in Mudimbe 190-91). V.Y. Mudimbe further sees "a spatial configuration" in imagining "a panoramic view of African *gnosis*" (191). Discussing space, therefore, involves a complexity of ontologies, cosmologies, and many other *systems* that it holds together or connects with.

In traditional Africa, land (a major component of space) is highly valued. Ngugi wa Thiongo in *Weep Not, Child* says of land among the Gikuyu people:

Any man who had land was considered rich. If a man had plenty of money, many motor cars, but no land, he could never be counted as rich. A man who went with tattered clothes but had at least an acre of red earth was better off than the man with money (22).

So space-bound on the physical plane is the African worldview that when old people die, they are expected to be taken to their home places for burial. It is as if the individual who was given his or her first nourishment in an area upon birth should return to the spiritual realm upon death through the same gateway in order to complete a life cycle.

My Urhobo people of the Niger Delta have the concept of *Urhoro*. It is the mythical place – paradoxically a-spatial – through which people in the spiritual world make their pre-natal choices and are then born into this world. Every individual, according to this mythical concept, is fated to live in accordance with his or her choice at *Urhoro*. In other words, we are predestined in the Urhobo worldview. Sometimes, according to elders of the group, sacrifices can be offered to ward off negative forces. There is, thus, traffic between the spiritual and physical worlds of the Niger Delta. When somebody dies, the person passes through the gate of *Urhoro* into the spiritual world to be an ancestor, who will be reborn again and again. Among the Urhobo, people talk of *this* world and the *next* world.

The Urhobo concept of *Urhoro* not only ties space to the physical and the spiritual, but also to the temporal and the a-temporal in the unending cycle of reincarnation. Nativity is significant here as the known and familiar each seeks its own kind. The Urhobo myth of *eda*, what the Yoruba and the Igbo respectively call *abiku* and *ogbanje*, can be anchored on this spiritual dimension of beliefs in my native Niger Delta home.

Urhoro appears directly and indirectly in my writing. A recent long poem is titled "Urhoro: Going in Cycles." In it I reflect not only on my personal condition and the impact of blood relations (daughter and father) on me but also on the human condition and the ironies involved:

> I who side-slipped every ambush on the road
> am bound to a survival kit,
> thrown into a rioting mass of currents.
> Buoyed by precedents of crossing rivers
> in *Olokun*'s arms, without a boat,
> I can understand why the champion swimmer

> drowns in a knee-depth, while
> the novice doomed to disappear
> escapes the shark bite of bad mouths.

Later in the same poem,

> I surrender my garments and property,
> but will not give up the bird
> that flies and flies, brightening
> my eyes beyond the horizon...

That "bird" is my soul with its possibilities that emanate from the place, from *Urhoro*, the outer and spiritual space of my native Niger Delta.

Space is more meaningful when seen through time. The singularity of reality lies in the connection of a point in space with a moment in time. As Mudimbe puts it, "all cultural figures determine their own specificity in apparently regional ruptures and continuities, whereby the otherness of their being appears as dynamic event, and thus history. All temporal pasts expose an otherness of the same ontological quality as the otherness unveiled by anthropologists" (195). Time transforms a place and accelerates its culture in the changes, which occur. Culture is thus dynamic. A place can expand or become narrow but the theoretical space remains even in memory if re-occupied. It is for these dynamics that culture and society are redefined by the transformation of space through human contact in time. Values of a people change, social and cultural icons also change. The creative writer finds himself or herself in the vortex of this socio-cultural flux set about by the impact of time on place.

The writer attempts to bridge time and space. He or she can only reflect, for the most part, the time of his or her existence. I see myself, if not consciously but subconsciously, as chronicling the time in which I live from the positionality of the Niger Delta. To put it differently but in a Chinua Achebe image, I am watching the masquerade of life from my Niger Delta foothold. This positioning no doubt presents advantages and disadvantages, because seeing things through this local but specific perspective could bring an intense vision. At the same time, narrowness to a specific place is bound to obscure some distant angles. To put this more bluntly, because of my Niger Delta nativity, I am subconsciously conditioned to respond to reality in a way unique to me and different from others who are strangers there. People who share the same birthplace are connected in their group values and interests. The Niger Delta is the three-dimensional space that time continues to change. As Nadezhda Mandelstam asks of the Russia of the Stalinist period, can I escape the Niger Delta? My life on earth started from here. If the purpose of life is to build, there is so much in the area to build upon. However, to avoid a constraining parochiality, the writer needs "friends and allies across barriers of both time and space" (Mandelstam 229); hence I open myself to other worlds. But significantly, the writer nourished by a specific place gives back something by assuming the responsibility of being an honest, sincere, and passionate witness of his place and time. If my writing in part reflects the *zeitgeist* and *volkgeist* of the Niger Delta, then I feel I have performed a duty. After all, the attributes of a place's culture are equivalent to the attributes of a period's culture.

A signifying icon of a place's culture is the prevailing pantheon. Of course, gods are indigenous to specific ethnic places. The Romans and Greeks had their gods with specific localities as their haunts. Homer and Ovid, among other classical writers, utilized the presence of gods with great effect. Closer home, Wole Soyinka demonstrates the power of one's people's gods in the creative writing process. *Idanre and Other Poems* and *Ogun Abibiman*, two poetry collections, have Ogun as the central "character." In fact, Ogun defines the poet's persona in Soyinka's poetry. Much of Soyinka's writing bristles with Yoruba gods. Chinua Achebe also refers to Igbo gods such as Ani, the Earth goddess, and Amadiora, god of thunder and lightning, in his writing.

Among the Urhobo people of the Niger Delta, devotees constantly invoke gods to help in difficult situations. Of these gods, four have always fascinated me and entered my writing. They are: *Uhaghwa*, god of songs; *Aridon*, god of memory; *Umalokun* or Mammy Water (called *Olokun* by others); and *Abadi/Ivwri*, god of war. Other Niger Delta groups like the Ijo and the Itsekiri also revere *Umalokun*, goddess of the waters and wealth. To a large extent, a people's gods help to define their spiritual concerns and worldview. In much of traditional Africa, gods are the apotheosization of a people's values, beliefs, and desires. The mystery of the large expanse of the sea instils awe among the Urhobo to worship its spirit. This spirit is the goddess of beauty and wealth that lives in a skyscraper of needles underwater. Such is the impact of the native god/dess that at my first physical contact with the

Pacific in the San Francisco-Sausalito Bay Area, I had to invoke *Umalokun*.

Gods have their homes but the efficacy of their influence, blessing, and power goes beyond their places of origin. In other words, there are no barriers to their power over their devotees. That is why a god's totem pet like the iguana will always be treated with reverence by the Orogun clan people of the Niger Delta in whatever part of the world they find one. *Uhaghwa* and *Aridon* are sometimes used interchangeably by Urhobo people and I have made *Aridon* assume the role of *Uhaghwa* and vice versa. I started with having *Uhaghwa* as my mentor god, hence the frequent invocation in my two early collections, *Children of Iroko and Other Poems* and *Labyrinths of the Delta*. I needed the inspiration of the god of songs then to fire me up. Later, as I grow older, memory has become more important to me and I have come to have *Aridon* as my other mentor. It is *Aridon* that I invoke in "The Fate of Vultures" to "blaze an ash-trail to the hands / that buried crates of cash in their bowels..." (*The Fate of Vultures*, 11). I now relate to the two gods as twin-gods and my mentors because I need inspiration and I need the memory to ground my experience.

While the Niger Delta is physical and geographical, it has a mythic dimension whose uniqueness of folklore is tapped by the native artist. Where else than in the riverine area of the Niger Delta will the tortoise/turtle become a major mythic figure? The tortoise has many names in the Urhobo language. It is *orose* (the shell one), *alauke* (the hunch-back), *oroghwuwevwiya* (the one that carries a house along), and *ogbeyin* (the cunning one). The so many attributes of the tortoise in Urhobo folklore involve cunning, greed, selfishness, and meanness. I have transferred the negative attributes of the tortoise to the corrupt Nigerian politicians and military dictators, who are so selfish that they do not care about how the nation suffers from their individual avarice. The Niger Delta myths are sources of allusions to describe the present reality of the Nigerian nation.

There are other examples of the Delta mythic world. There is the *oko* drumming bird, which comes with the early heavy rains that turn the dry creeks into tumultuous currents that flow into the big rivers that pour themselves into the Atlantic Ocean. "Going to the sea" in Urhobo and Ijo suggests death and entering eternity. There is the belief similar to the Greeks' about the dead being ferried across the sea into the spirit world. A pioneer Niger Delta poet, J.P. Bekederemo-Clark, uses this image in *A Reed in the Tide*.

The mythic corpus of the Niger Delta infuses poetry and other creative writings with a ready storehouse of allusions, which root the poetic vision in a specific culture, locus, and reality. It gives energy and mystical glamour to the creative work.

The Niger Delta as a cultural home has its imprints on languages. By its exposure to the outside world by way of the demarcating Atlantic Ocean, this area has always been in dialogue or conflict over time with other cultures, especially the Western/European culture. This again is testimony that a culture though with a spatial setting is not contained by spatial boundaries. The infusion of European languages and neologisms into Urhobo and other local languages and the emergence of Pidgin English are strong indications of the openness of *any* place to foreign influences.

The Urhobo area has its socio-cultural life stamped with early European influence. The Portuguese were the first Europeans to trade with people of the Niger Delta. The Urhobo call them "Potukri" and for a long time called Europeans irrespective of their national origin "Potukri." From the colonial period, the Europeans started to be called "oyibo." The "oyibo" has a negative connotation because of slave trade, colonialism, and other forms of European exploitation and domination of Africans. Many Urhobo words today are neologisms or rather Urhoboizing of Portuguese. The following Urhobo words show the Niger Delta's indebtedness to Portuguese: *oro* (gold), *ughojo* (wristwatch/clock), *osete* (plate), *ukujere* (spoon), *meje* (table), *sabato* (shoes), and *isama* (salmon/canned fish).

There is also indebtedness to English. The Urhobo word for sailor is *kruman*, the Urhoboization of "crewman." The Urhobo names of many modern technological items are basically English with a local accent. Words for airplane, radio, television, video, motor car, and many others are transparently English-derived. Other influences of the European incursion include the bringing of the "wrapper" dress, which has become a cultural costume of the Niger Delta people. The fabric for this dress originated from Goa/India and brought first as a means of exchange by the Portuguese and later by the British in the barter trade between Europeans and Africans. Niger Delta people acted as "middle-men" between the Europeans and the hinterland groups such as the Igbo and Bini.

Pidgin English in Nigeria was for a long time a Delta monopoly. Sapele and Warri in the present-day Delta State and Port Harcourt in Rivers State are the bastions of Pidgin English. Of course, these cities are ports in which there was a lot of exchange between Europeans and Africans. Pidgin English in Warri and Sapele has absorbed Urhobo semantics and syntax in its unique "broken English."

I have a few poems in Urhobo and Pidgin English respectively. Part of "The Wrestler" is in Urhobo, a song, which begins and ends the poem. However, even when the poems are written in English, the major symbols and rhythms are derived from Urhobo experience. A poem like "The Battle" will make its greatest impact on an Urhobo speaker than on others:

> For fear of exposing its soft body
> the *oghighe* plant covers itself with thorns,
> for fear of bad company
> the *akpobrisi* keeps distant from other trees,
> for fear of falling into the grip of age
> the python yearly casts off its skin,
> for fear of its head
> the tortoise moves inside a fortress.
> For fear of our lives
> we arm in diverse ways
> to fight the same battle.
> (*The Endless Song*, 44).

As I stated in "Musical Roots: The Rhythm of Modern African Poetry," many African poets superimpose English/foreign language words over native rhythmic patterns. In such cases, "a poem's rhythm is lifted or distorted from an existing traditional musical composition" (Ojaide 67). Thus, when I write about the turtle/tortoise in "Labyrinths of the Delta," the title poem of the collection, I am in fact building a poem on an Urhobo folktale's song. Here's the folksong:

> *Uro bio ogbeyin rhe* / Currents, bring back the turtle
> *Tue tue* / Steadily, steadily
> *Uro bio ogbeyin rhe* / Currents, bring back the turtle
> *Tue tue* / Steadily, steadily
> *Ogbeyin ruvwe* / Turtle has hurt me
> *Oru vwa abo vwirhin* / it broke my hands
> *Tue tue* / Steadily, steadily
> *Ogbeyin ruvwe* / Turtle has hurt me

> *Oru vwa awo vwirhin* / It broke my legs
> *Tue tue* /Steadily, steadily
> *Uro bio ogbeyin rhe* / Currents, bring back the turtle
> *Tue tue* / Steadily, steadily
> *Uro bio ogbeyin rhe* / Currents, bring back the turtle
> *Tue tue* / Steadily, steadily

Here is the rendition in a part of my poem:

> Turn the tortoise back, O Waters
> Bring him back
> Spare him mishap on the way
> Bring him back to me;
> He broke not only my hands
> But also my legs and ribs;
> Bring him back to me
> Spare him mishap on the way here
> And let the villain taste
> What he inflicted on me
> From my own hands (26).

Here the Urhobo characterization of the turtle becomes the symbol of exploitation and oppression for which the speaker seeks revenge and restitution.

I have learned much from an Urhobo poetic form, the *udje* dance song. A unique form that combines the dirge and the abuse song forms, the *udje* dance song is popular in the Ujevwen and Udu clans of Urhoboland. I have especially borrowed its satirical side and rhythm in my political poems. The *udje* dance song is a ready tool for me to use against the corrupt politicians and dictators of Nigeria and Africa. The indirection of naming what is generally known, the fictionalizing of facts, and the sharp edge of the criticism of the *udje* dance song form have informed such poems as "The Fate of Vultures," "State Executive," "Players," and the Ogiso poems in *Cannons for the Brave*.

In one of my published Pidgin English poems, "I Be Somebody," I try to use the common people's lingua franca to articulate and assert the dignity of the common person. Here's the poem:

> I fit shine your shoe like new one from supermarket,
> so I know something you no know for your life.

> I fit carry load for head from Lagos go Abuja,
> so I get power you think na only you get.
> If you enter my room, my children reach Nigerian Army;
> so I rich pass you, whether your naira full bank or house.
> You no know kindness, big man: na me de help
> push your car from gutter for rain, not for money at all;
> and you de splash poto-poto for my body when you de pass.
> To tell the truth, I get nothing; but
> you no fit get anything without poor man –
> na me be salt for the soup you de chop every day;
> I be nobody and I be somebody.
> (*The Eagle's Vision*, 69).

With the examples of my writing in Urhobo, imbibing Urhobo folklore and rhythms, and use of Pidgin English, the writer could be seen simultaneously as both the socio-cultural product and standard-bearer of his or her birthplace. The quality of the product depends on the individual talent of the writer, which is quite another matter.

The interplay of spatiality and time, which brings transformations in culture and society, shows in the material resources available to the writer. The change from the Niger Delta of my youth in the 1950s to the Delta of the 1990s exacerbates the tension in my poetry. There is the image of the past, which is drastically different from that of today, an idyllic past opposed to the ecologically tainted Westernized present. The opposition of the traditional Niger Delta and the modern Delta gives rise to two seemingly different "spaces" of my birthplace. Mudimbe poses the questions: "In which sense does the so-called traditional arrangement define itself as an autonomous field outside of modernity and vice-versa? In which mode of being are the concepts of tradition and modernity expressed and formulated within a cultural area?" (189) He gives no answers but suggests that local customs can be transformed by modern systems for the better.

I have nostalgia for the Niger Delta of my youth. I spent all my formative years in my native Delta home. Living with my maternal grandmother, my guardian angel Amreghe, I followed my grandpa and uncles to fish before I started to go with my own age-mates, Iboyi and Godwin, to fish with hooks. I followed adults in the family to "harvest" ponds. From these activities I understood why the earthworm used as bait in fishing is often compared to a woman who likes only soft spots. I knew the mudfish that enters the cone-shaped net as the figurative language for sex. I saw the beautiful *erhuvwudjayorho* fish, so beautiful but denied growing big, a sort of mystical law of compensation. In the creeks and rivers, there was a parade of fishes. There was the *onyenye* with an inimitable beauty. The swordfish, electric fish, snake-like fish (*ogbene*), *okpogun, obo,* and a variety of fresh and salt-water fish.

There were also the water lilies (*tetebe*) that grew on water, so delicate and so the metaphor for the resilience of a fragile being. Of course, gourds stood on top of fierce currents. By the later 1950s we heard of Gamalin 20 with greedy fishers who poisoned the fish to pick. Some cocoa farmers in Urhoboland had converted the chemical from being sprayed on cocoa plants to protect them from being destroyed by diseases to poisoning fish in ponds. The local bylaws banning fishing and palm-nut collecting at certain times of the year were still in place.

I followed the men to clear and plant the farms and watched the ritual of spraying the earth on the yam pieces and praying for fruitfulness before the planting. Every year brought its own demands, but the images of increase and fertility were always invoked. I heard the *apiapia* bird ushering in a new planting season with its song:

> *Ukpe tere* / Another year has come
> *Udu ko bruvwe* / And my heart beats
> *Kpe kpe* / In fear of the future.

I discovered that the python slept deeply and even when decapitated did not die immediately but only after noon when it would jerk before dying. No wonder my Grandma sometimes called me a python when I overslept and risked getting to school late. In the forest there was the man-like anthill (*orato*) with a helmet-like head. What of the civet cat (*aghwaghwa*) crying at night, the fear of the gorilla then said to rape beautiful women who went to farm alone? Even animals, one *udje* dance song states, know the difference between beautiful and ugly women! Thus, the waters and the land of the Niger Delta were invaluable resources that sustained the population.

The great change came with the arrival of Shell-BP, the oil-drilling multinational, in the Niger Delta about 1958. In the Urhobo area we heard of Shell's simultaneous presence in Oloibiri, Bonny, and other eastern parts of Ijoland. My childhood memoir, *Great Boys: Years of Childhood*, and a collection of poems on the impact of modern Western technology on traditional African life, *Daydreams of Ants*, deal with the post-Shell presence with its increasing ecological degradation of the

Niger Delta. Oil pipes broke and the waters once teeming with fish were polluted and many turned into dead creeks and rivers, which sent fishermen and women out of work. In many areas, including Kokori and Ughelli, Shell flared gas. The staple crops such as yams and cassava wilted. The heat killed the fauna and flora and possibly gave diseases to people who met untimely deaths. The catalogue of Shell's destruction of the environment with its adverse effects on inhabitants of the Niger Delta is endless.

The Niger Delta I once knew as home has changed drastically. The demise of the pristine environment has driven people from rural areas to the cities of Warri and Port Harcourt. The traditional occupations of farming, fishing, and hunting that used to sustain rural dwellers have been wiped out by oil drilling. Shell-BP and other oil corporations in Warri and Port Harcourt have become leading employers in the Niger Delta.

The new wealth brought by these oil companies has changed the socio-cultural lives of the people. The cramping of people in the cities brings its loosening of the traditional values that once governed the people's lives. Now modern urban lifestyles are prevalent: robbery, adultery, greed, and exploitation of others for personal gain.

The oil-boom of Nigeria in the late 1960s and 1970s exacerbated another aspect of the Niger Delta people; hence they call it the "oil doom" period. As a minority in the Nigerian federation, they feel cheated not only by the oil corporations but also by the Federal Government dominated by majority groups who are united in their exploitation and oppression of minority groups. Many Delta people believe that the Nigerian nation still stands as one only because of the abundance of oil in their area. The story of Nigeria would be different today if the oil were located in one of the three ethnic group areas of Hausa, Yoruba, and Ibo. In any case, the revenue allocation formula, which favours other groups at the expense of the Niger Delta people, is cause of deep-rooted resentment. The personal enrichment of national leaders and the development of other areas as the Delta deteriorated have made the minority Delta people more activist in both drawing attention to their sorry plight and calling for compensation. It is in light of this unconscionable anomaly that I wrote "Ughelli" in the late 1970s. The poem reads:

> To see her dry-skinned when her oil rejuvenates hags
> to leave her in darkness when her fuel lights the universe

to starve her despite all her produce
to let her dehydrate before the wells bored into her heart
to have her naked despite her innate industry
to keep her without roads when her sweat tars the outside world
to make her homeless when her idle neighbours inhabit skyscrapers
to see her lonely when sterile ones use her offspring as servants
to regard the artisan as a non-person when drones celebrate with her
    sweat,

for the palm's oil to be called the fig tree's
for the goddess of wealth not to be complimented for her gifts
but spat upon by raiders of her bosom
for one to earn so much and be denied all except life –
robbery wears a thousand masks in official bills –
and for her to be sucked anaemic by an army of leeches,
    it is a big shame(74).

In the 1960s and 1970s, Ughelli was not just the administrative headquarters of Urhobo East local government but the centre of an oil-producing area. The town had no electricity (and pipe-borne water) while it supplied the rest of the country immense revenue and electric power. The same Ughelli whose gas is said to be about the best in the world!

Today the Niger Delta as space/place of oil and minority status in the Nigerian nation has generated ideas of struggle and survival among its people. In then Rivers State (now Rivers and Bayelsa States), Isaac Adaka Boro struggled against regional and national exploitation before his death. The Nigerian civil war was fought for the soul of the Niger Delta because of its huge oil reserves as both parties had their eyes on the "prize," oil. The problems of Boro's time have been made worse by the alliance of multinational corporations and military dictatorship. Ken Saro-Wiwa's struggle for the Ogoni and other minority groups of the Niger Delta is consequent upon the pollution, deprivation, exploitation and neglect of the oil-producing area, synonymous with the Niger Delta. Saro-Wiwa's struggle was for the just compensation of the people for the wealth taken away by Shell and the Nigerian Government, while their birthplace was being destroyed irrevocably by oil spillage, gas flaring, and other forms of pollution. Saro-Wiwa called for investment in the area to correct the ecological destruction suffered over decades because of oil exploration. The Movement for the

Survival of the Ogoni People (MOSOP) represents the temperament of the Niger Delta people.

The Niger Delta gives identity to its natives. The inhabitants of this watery land of lush vegetation are a minority in the Nigerian federation with a very strong center that has access to all resources within its frontiers. The status of these minorities is that of an exploited people. It is for this reason that one of the Delta writer's orientation is to signify the Delta, showing its paradox of sitting on oil and yet remaining impoverished.

Different as the Niger Delta is, it is connected with others. I have already discussed the impact of the European connection on Urhobo language and culture. But even earlier and after the European incursion, there has always been a strong African connection. The Urhobo people trace their roots to Benin and Ife, further inland. The Itsekiri whose language is very close to a Yoruba dialect trace their royalty to somewhere else. The Ijo appear to be the only group that has always been there, since they have no myths or legends of coming from elsewhere to their present abode and other groups like the Urhobo and Itsekiri met them there. Igbo and Edo words appear in Urhobo language and this suggests influence and contact. In the case of Edo, the Urhobo, Bini, Ishan, and some other groups might have once lived in an eponymous place called Aka before dispersing to their present locations. In modern times, Warri and Port Harcourt, the two major Niger Delta cities, have become very cosmopolitan in absorbing people of different groups from different places into the Delta community. Apart from Lagos, Warri and Port Harcourt could boast of having the largest population of Europeans and Americans in Nigeria.

The Niger Delta is not just physical space but a spiritual, mystical, and psychological setting. It evokes ideas of public and private space in me: the physical and the psychic Delta, which are fused in my individual being. I foreground the Delta both consciously and unconsciously; consciously because it is the place I know best and I am most familiar with and unconsciously because I have so imbibed its spirit that it speaks in me even when I am not aware of it. It is the backcloth, so to say, of my experiences as a writer. It is the context of the text of my writing. The Niger Delta provides me different types of refuge, defence, and guard. This only means that nativity of a place can run deep in one's psyche and perspective. Arguably, it can also be a constraint, if not mitigated by a readiness to accept what will nourish and reinforce it from other cultures. The Niger Delta is unique in its rootedness but also has by its position as the marine gateway to Nigeria absorbed European and African influences. Nativity brings into tension "ours" and "theirs" in values and interests as an exploited minority in the majority-dominated Nigerian polity. However, the Delta area has shown how Sameness does not preclude the Other.

From my discussion so far it is apparent that space and time are inter-related. The Niger Delta has history, an indication of a common experience of a people over time. If "history is a relation to values and sets itself on mechanisms of intellectual valorization" (Mudimbe192), my vision is colored by the history of the Niger Delta. There have been changes from a traditional idyllic place to a modern area rifled with oil-drilling businesses. The historical inter-relationship between space as place, culture, and society poses challenges of nativity to me as a writer. There is a psychic transference onto Urhobo and the Niger Delta of the past into the present. With the pivotal role of memory in the creative process of writing poetry, nativity is a continuous presence that keeps the flame of associations burning. I see much of the world and life through the eyes of a Niger Delta indigene. My vision emanates from where I *stand*.

The minority people have moved from natural contentment to political agitation against exploitation. The demand by the old Delta Province to become a state of its own without Anioma is another indication of the politicization of nativity. In Delta State, the inhabitants of the old Delta Province see themselves as the true Delta people! If this coincides with a shift from poetry of nature invocation to that of political activism, it only means that nativity has so much power on the writer.

There is an accumulation of forces deriving from the particular nature and condition of the place. The Delta is a body of place and a spirit. I am not an air-plant. I may travel the world and live elsewhere but I am physically and psychically anchored to the Niger Delta. It is the driving spirit of the Delta that shapes the vision and provides the images in my writing.

In conclusion, and to borrow Wall on Hurston, wherever I journey, I am able to draw on the Urhobo Niger Delta heritage and find strength to remain myself (27). My sense of home is based on a multiplicity of factors, my persona rooted in the Niger Delta of the 1950s to the present. Whether I am physically displaced from home, I am intuitively linked to my home, which I can reclaim effortlessly. In other words, place is not only physical but mental, spiritual, and psychic. My outside experiences stretch the parameters of my homeland intellectually. The Niger Delta moulds my identity at home and outside, as in many ways I am one with its people. Nostalgia for this land of evergreen rain forests persists in me. I can always image an inner space filled with pieces from everywhere but dominated and coloured by the Niger Delta which strengthens my bond with humanity.

Coming Home

I might disembark at more ports than
the moon can cope with in a full phase.
I might bring new mirrors to elders,
that breed of tenacious roots who prefer
an interpreter of two languages to recast
their own son's tales of his recent sojourn.
I might be the migrant bird that
shores up the seasons in the calendar.
I might be current finding my way
from mountain to sea, not the river's bed.
I would not be the ship mocking the rock
because it has freedom of movement,
nor would I be the rock mocking the ship
because it does not yield to anybody's craft.

At home every proverb becomes a tonic
that fortifies through jungle cities abroad,
every bird or animal proffers tales of
how to move in the minefield of America;
every native cherry flavours the tongue
with straight face smiles of my childhood –
erased, the aftertaste of not just Diet Coke
but also the toxic breath of smokers.
Every face home, brother or sister;
my gods worship their devotees!

Now silent from the last summons,
Ishaka never breached the clan's walls;
yet spun stories of faraway places –
glass towers, beauties, and monsters;

details gave truth to the scatterbrain.
But who, reeling with laughter and longing
for England, cared about his running mad?
His stories of London launched me on
the fountain-pen trail to meet the Queen.
I might be Odysseus' son in another life,
lost more than one love to absence
and gained one away to take home;
still I would love to be a home fellow
powered by the draughts I imbibe.

Elders talk of "Two mouths, one stomach."
I have not yet encountered the strange one
but have given it a place in memory-yard,
the only charming monster in the world.
Coming home we exchange gifts and tales,
each more fond of the other's special fortune –
alliance of *iroko* and eagle in a divine bond.
And two firm hands lift the calabash
from the ground to the mouth
to slake the parched body!

(May 25, 1994)

References and works cited

Achebe, Chinua. *Things Fall Apart*. London: Heinemann, 1958.
Clark-Bekederemo, John Pepper. *A Reed in the Tide*. London: Longman, 1965.
---. *Casualties*. London: Longman, 1970.
Danto, Arthur C. *Narrative and Knowledge*. New York: Columbia UP, 1985.
Johnson, Barbara. "Response" in Houston A. Baker, Jr. and Patricia Redmond, eds. *Afro-American Literary Study in the 1990s*. Chicago: U of Chicago Press, 1989.
Mandelstam, Nadezhda. *Hope Against Hope*. New York: Atheneum, 1970.
---. *Hope Abandoned*. New York: Atheneum, 1974.
Mbiti, John S. *African Religions and Philosophy*. Oxford: Heinemann, 1969.
Mudimbe, V.Y. *The Invention of Africa: Gnosis, Philosophy, and the Order of Knowledge*. Bloomington and Indianapolis: Indiana UP, 1988.
Ngugi, wa Thiongo. *Weep Not, Child*. London: Heinemann, 1964.

---. *Petals of Blood*. London: Heinemann, 1977.
Ojaide, Tanure. *Children of Iroko and Other Poems*. New York: Greenfield Review Press, 1973.
---. *Labyrinths of the Delta*. New York: Greenfield Review Press, 1986.
---. *The Eagle's Vision*. Detroit: Lotus Press, 1987.
---. *The Endless Song*. Lagos: Malthouse Press, 1989.
---. *The Fate of Vultures*. Lagos: Malthouse Press, 1990.
---. *The Blood of Peace*. Oxford: Heinemann, 1991.
---. "Musical Roots: The Rhythm of Modern African Poetry," *The Middle-Atlantic Writers Association Review*, Vol. 7, No. 2 (December 1992).
---. *Cannons for the Brave*. Lagos: Malthouse Press, 1996 (forthcoming).
Soyinka, Wole. *Idanre and Other Poems*. London: Eyre Methuen, 1967.
---. *A Shuttle in the Crypt*. London: Collings/Methuen, 1972.
---. *Ogun Abibiman*. London: Rex Collings, 1978.
---. *Myth, Literature and the African World*. Cambridge: Cambridge UP, 1976.
Wall, Cheryl A. *Women of the Harlem Renaissance*. Bloomington/Indianapolis: Indiana UP, 1985.

IV

African culture today[*]

At 47 I feel I have experienced two hundred or more years of African history. In the last few decades, there has been an acceleration of changes that make me fear for my people's way of life. I have seen the traditional ways lose their grip on people to new ways that threaten old identities. From my own experience, our environment has so changed that history appears to have leaped and somersaulted. In fact, things are moving with their heads; their legs in the air. Some witch's craft has impaled the old culture we were all proud of. Before long the known and familiar of my childhood days would be gone. In their places, alien ways that could make their adherents rootless beings. And yet I am a child of the *iroko* tree that stands firm and tall in the forest! I see no efforts to arrest the great erosion that is under way.

I, Big Bone to my village elders when I had barely left the cradle, have surprised myself. What fortune-teller that my anxious grandmother or mother consulted would have seen this far ahead? Who could have divined that I would not only survive the hunchback's witchcraft, but would have the fountain-pen as a wand, and after Grandma's and Father's deaths travel even farther than they could possibly have imagined?

An Urhobo saying readily comes to mind. Who travels wide sees more than who lives long in one place. Time and space have always been central to Urhobo worldview and their intersection in me has left a vision of a vanishing culture. I want to use my Urhobo experience as a starting point to reflect on African culture today.

My father met my mother during the solar eclipse of 1947. It was a phenomenon even the oldest in the clan had not witnessed. It caught

---

[*] Written in 1995 as part of a cultural dialogue with Fred Will

everybody by surprise. Many had felt the world had come to an end, a sort of cosmic ambush that no warrior people could escape. But they were relieved after some fifteen minutes, the sky cleared and returned to its daylight familiarity. They had a new lease of life that new ways would assault and nibble away. Today many things I knew as a child have become shadows of their former selves. Grandma in her present incarnation would be a shadow of her old self, if she were to have knowledge of her former lives!

I am a product of vigorous loins and the Big Womb. That was the year after the eclipse, 1948. My first four years were lived in a village lost in the forest and whose name I had not even known until I made inquiries recently. It was always referred to as the old village; nobody ever called its real name. It was as if the abandoned should be forgotten. However, it was there, by Grandpa's pepper-fruit plant, that my birth cord was buried. That old homestead saw nothing of modernity. I can still recall the homes roofed with thatches; a community in which everybody knew each other. That was not my father's place; it was my mother's place. Boys among my people seek refuge in their mothers' home-places. My father calculated right and time would tell that his judgement was very sound.

Both in the old village and later at Oko-Ibada, I did not miss my father. My uncles, aunts, and the entire adult population of relatives took me as their very own. My uncles did not pay special attention to their biological children. I even had an advantage as I was called to eat by each of them. At Christmas and traditional festivals, I could brag with an array of gifts, especially clothes. Grandma Amreghe, my guardian angel, forever thoughtful of my good, sometimes gave out from my portion to other children whose fathers were there so that they would not be jealous of me. I was a stranger, a guest, who had to be well taken care of. Okpoto, my uncle's first son, remains my own brother till today.

Then when four or thereabouts the entire village moved into a newly founded one, Oko-Ibada. It was by a motorable road and in place of thatch roofs, the homes had corrugated iron sheets. Bicycles were many and instead of bush paths, laterite and wider roads. Road workers maintained the road and I heard of PWD even before I was literate. The Public Works Department kept the roads in good condition. The first "motor" that came to the village created quite a commotion as later the sight of Shell-BP's gas flares at night. The lorry came to pick dry rubber sheets from my uncle, Otata. Government tax collectors came not long after the first sacrifice at the centre of the village, before an *oghighe* plant. This was always planted at the centre of a habitation, according to Urhobo custom. Tax collectors were like a scourge, and male adults fled at the least hint of their appearance. Women did not pay taxes then. On few occasions, children were held hostage by the tax collectors and were only released after their parents had come out of hiding to pay their taxes.

National politics started to be felt. The Cock and the Palm Tree, the National Council of Nigeria and Cameroon and the Action Group respectively divided a peaceful village. You had to belong to one or the other. You were either for Zik of Africa or for Awo, the champion of free education. The white man who had been ruling us had to be kicked out for our national independence in 1960. I had gone to St. Charles's Elementary School at Okurekpo when five and got turned back for being too small. At six I was admitted and despite my being called Emoghware, son of Dafetanure, son of Ojaide, I was given another name – Moses. Later I was baptized with the name of Moses in the Catholic Church. I had no idea of what people I was going to lead to freedom! Once I left elementary school for secondary school at Obinomba in the Ukwani (Igbo) area, I was in the open world; not just among the Urhobo people, but among other groups.

I was to complete my undergraduate studies before Oko-Ibada moved to Okurekpo, another village but on the tarred road between Warri and Onitsha. We lived by the "garage," an intersection of the main tarred road and the untarred road from Okpara Inland to Okpara Waterside. The movement from Oko-Igberhe to Oko-Ibada and then to Okurekpo before I went to work in Warri, the oil city, is a metaphor for my experience of African culture. It was a movement from the forest to a clearing, from darkness to light, from traditionalism to modernity, from refuge to exposure.

Oko-Igberhe was a pristine environment. The people got whatever they needed for sustenance from around them. The village was by streams and creeks. Only Urhobo was spoken there. Almost everybody fished, despite other occupations like palm nut collecting, farming, or rubber tapping. The same held true in Oko-Ibada. My mother (in her frequent visits) and my uncle's wives went to fish with *ayaro* scoop nets and caught crayfish and others. They caught just enough for the specific meals they wanted to prepare. My uncles and Grandpa set their *ige* nets for mudfish and catfish in the creeks and streams. I set hooks and caught different types of fish.

Yams, coco-yams, and cassava were planted. Hunting was done during the day and at night. Men and young ones also set traps to catch bush animals. My Grandma, who lived to about ninety, told me she never experienced famine all her life. That was when I told her about the drought and famine in some African countries I read in papers about 1973. The people knew how to balance nature, as they did not over-crop the land and streams. So they had their own conservation methods. There were seasons for palm nut collecting. You could not fish in ponds in the dry season. A heavy fine was imposed on whoever broke the ban.

Of course, Oko-Igberhe and Oko-Ibada were more inside than Okurekpo, but the three villages espoused moral and ethical codes different from Warri's, the modern Westernized city that is claimed by Urhobo, Ijo, and Itsekiri as theirs. In the villages adults taught children ethics and morality after the day's work at the "fire-side school" with folktales, myths, legends, epics, proverbs, puzzles, and other traditional tropes. Stealing was extremely rare and if it occurred and the person caught, he or she was shamed as a determent for others. The thief would beat a drum through the main street announcing the crime committed.

Sex was for married adults or male adults and their concubines. Every adult married. Or, he or she was at least expected to get married. People suspected the unmarried men. I never knew of an adult woman who was not married, who had not once married, or not related romantically to a man. Every man and woman could be identified by their marital status – this man's wife, this woman's husband or friend. Men could marry several wives if they could afford it, but many had one or two. Polygamy was more of economic consideration than an expression of sexual prowess. Husbands and wives made love at night in the privacy of the man's bed. Stories of uncontrolled love were told for fun. There was a man who could not wait till night and approached his wife who had just come back from a cassava farm, sweating and hungry. The woman protested, but the man had his way! The man was condemned, as there ought to be some decency to sexual intercourse. People wondered when night watchmen slept with their wives! The unmarried were not supposed to make love but some youths did that behind the plantain plants in the dark or when playing on moonlit nights.

Every first-born is, according to custom, a traditional priest in Urhobo. I saw Grandpa Odjegba perform his duties as a priest, as my uncle Onosigho. I am *omowaran*, and as a first-born had to serve in traditional sacrifices. Becoming a Christian and serving at Mass as I did for four years in secondary school did not absolve me from my traditional firstborn responsibilities. Chickens, goats, and meals were offered as sacrifices to ancestors and gods. I am still expected today to offer sacrifices to my deceased father. As a child, I was wherever there was to be a sacrifice in the village. There was always plenty of food to eat. The child that follows the medicine-man or elders to sacrifice always has enough to eat! As young ones, we cleaned the sacrificed animals or birds and helped to prepare the delicious *ukodo* thick soup used for sacrifice. Traditional annual festivals were anxiously awaited because of the mandatory sacrifices during the period. They were occasions to have our fill of sumptuous dishes.

Shell-British Petroleum came about 1958 to prospect for oil and got a lot of it and gas. Oil they sold, gas they flared before us. The inroads of whites and townspeople into the rural area strained the values of our people. Of course, the value of money increased considerably. Townspeople treated money like a god – they adored it. This god intoxicated like wine when they had a lot of it. Women were seduced and some eloped with townspeople never to be heard of again. Money was more powerful than love! The married women in Warri and the few in the villages who flirted with other men said the ancestors and gods did not understand English and so they were not intimidated from having their hearts' content! Stealing, as in Warri, became more frequent even in Okurekpo. Shell-BP tore open not just the physical environment but turned upside down many of the values the people had held sacrosanct. The frequent cases of oil spillage and the gas flaring destroyed rivers, creeks, farmlands, and lives – how many dying of unknown new diseases ever thought of the European witchcraft of oil-drilling and its attendant pollution?

Today African culture has changed drastically. Change is inevitable but one should fear the change for the worse. My personal experience reflects the changes. Once at Okpara Waterside, pontoons and other watercraft used to sail in to take away bales of rubber sheets from the factory there. The River Ethiope there then, as at Sapele, was open. Today it is reduced to a quarter of its width. This in about thirty years or less! The river has shrunk not just because of the water hyacinth alone. Rivers, streams, and creeks in the Niger Delta have not only been covered with silts but have been clogged by only-God-knows-what. They are no longer passable. I don't know where those boats that were common in my youth are now. The wide Ethiope River at Sapele that enabled the car-carrying pontoon to cross has shrunk to about twenty yards. There were times in history that Portuguese and later slave-trading boats used to pass Agbarho, but the river there is shrivelled to a thin sheet that can barely take a dugout.

All the waterlogged lands are now dry. Water has been "driven" away because of the pressure of population explosion. More people, more houses. More people, more land to be reclaimed. The planting of rubber after World War I in much of Urhobo is also blamed for the disappearance of water. The wealth of fish in the water and of animals in the bush has gone. Gas-flaring, oil spillage and other forms of pollution have destroyed the fishes, animals, crops, and plants. People have moved from the villages, which can no longer sustain them, as their means of livelihood have been destroyed or threatened. There is malnutrition both in the village and in the city. How things have changed! Warri is teeming with people like one endless open market.

My father's major concern about my safety in his lifetime was that the hunchback, whose praise-name was *Aeroplane*, should not cast an evil spell on me. She was known as a witch and my father feared her cousin more than any plague you could imagine. She died before my father. Ironically, it was an airplane that bore me to the West, first to Syracuse, New York. The airplane would later be my commuter craft. It was the airplane that brought me to Iowa City to participate in the International Writing Program, whose co-director Fred Will became my friend. It is with him that I engage in this dialogue – Africa and the West. Now he knows where I come from.

I consider myself a perfect reflection of African culture today. My experience also demonstrates the love-hate but inseparable relationship between Africa and the West, especially America. As we enter another century, this relationship has become more precarious in its imbalance. The West has so much self-interest that it does not want the good of others. It can argue that without its contact, Africa would still be in the Stone Age. Furthermore, it would argue that it is doing its best with the World Bank and the International Monetary Fund to pull Africa out of its abysmal debts. Africa would have liked to be left alone from the beginning to develop in its own way. Once you incapacitate somebody, as Africa was done through slave trade and colonialism, there is little that can be done in later life to reverse the situation. Not all wrongs can be turned right. Africans fear Westerners even when they bring "gifts" like the loans and recommendations of the IMF and the World Bank, which have made them to sink deeper into inhuman misery as the European world capitalists achieved higher standards of living. The contradictions of European world impact continue to dog Africans.

I currently live in Dayberry Lane in the Birnam Woods area of Charlotte in North Carolina. The neighborhood streets I walk and drive through daily are Shakespearean: Falstaff, Othello, Portia, Touchstone, Dunsinane, Viola, Henry IV, and Faulconbridge, among so many others. How could anybody have foreseen thirty years ago when I took the Shakespeare course from the Scottish McVeagh that I would live in Birnam Woods quarter of a Queen City? I read A.C. Bradley's *Shakespearean Tragedy* thoroughly as I did Wilson Knight's essays on the English bard. Those courses prepared me for where I am today.

The irony of a modern African poet living in North Carolina is never lost on me. Living in a former slave state represented in the American Senate by, of all people, the ultra conservative Jesse Helms! The name speaks for itself. That he gets re-elected also speaks something loud.

I am in a double bind. I know the ideal thing is for me to be living in Nigeria. Be in the war-front against military dictatorship. Be under crossfire in the war against injustice and poverty. Participate in the hydra-headed war against underdevelopment. But I am here in North Carolina. I must have a strong reason to endure the Carolinian blue, which for all appearances gave rise to the blues of African Americans that I still hear in the streets.

My first daughter has sickle cell anaemia and suffers from spastic paralysis. She was very normal when we lived in Syracuse. Until she was seven in Maiduguri, where the doctors said her blood count was high enough and okay despite her getting pale because of the sickling of her red blood corpuscles. She gradually became helpless and lost her walking ability. Later in Walla Walla, Washington, and in Charlotte, we would learn that she suffered multiple mild strokes while in Nigeria. We knew that she fell at school in Maiduguri but the University Teaching Hospital, the centre of excellence in name, did not report any finding despite the many tests.

Nigeria has no policy on the disabled. In the mainly Muslim North, most of the disabled turn up after sunrise at street intersections, departmental stores, and other public places. They shake their tin bowls singing songs that exhort the generous giver. Being disabled and begging are seen as synonymous. Different forms of disability are exhibited. The blind form a majority because they live in the region of a blinding disease that the World Health Organization has been helping to combat. The crippled are also many. All forms of deformities, including stumps of lost arms or legs, are flaunted at you. You have to see before you believe and give out of pity! They put in so much stamina into the chanting and scrambling that they sweat profusely. Just before sundown, before the muezzins call for the evening prayer, they vanish for the day. Many of such professional beggars are rumoured to be rich; in fact richer than the workers who give them money.

In much of the southern part of Nigeria, the disabled are invisible. They are confined to their family homes, as if their existence is a disgrace to the family. I understand that when mothers delivered deformed babies or they got disabled, they were secretly stifled to death. This murder was rare but an open secret, which only meant that there was tacit approval of the action. It was only in one or two places like the Oji River area of the defunct Biafra, after the civil war, that there was some attempt to make the disabled to live meaningful lives.

There are exceptions to the blind and the crippled begging for a living. In Edafe Village there was the cripple Okpreku, who had so much energy and covered many miles to social occasions. He always joked that his legs were not firm, but he had hands whose strength could match those of ten people. He was a comedian who made fun of his condition and was highly admired for his acceptance of fate and for his courage. He had his own farms, married, and had several children. There was also the famous cripple of Ekrerhavwen, the best-known rope-maker and basket-weaver in all Urhobo in his days. And in my maternal family, Ishaka married Ematije, who had only the left hand. Mother of my boyhood friend, Iboyi, I never asked whether she was born so or sustained an injury later in life. But Ematije was the heroine of Oko-Ibada. She farmed, grated her cassava, and weeded her farm like a giant. Her one hand was stronger than ten other right hands combined. I was witness to what was said to be her only fight. A woman tested her patience beyond reason. This woman openly insulted Ematije for having only one hand. The culture forbids that. Disability is not chosen but inflicted by fate. Ematije kicked and punched the errant woman to bleed, cry, and flee from her steel left hand.

Since we came back to the United States, Western medicine and technology have been helping my daughter to live with some dignity. She has two wheelchairs, one motorized and the other manual. A school bus comes every school day to take her to her East Mecklenburg high school and brings her back at 3.30 p.m. almost regularly. Every school is supposed to be wheelchair accessible. The American Disability Act recommends measures that have to be taken in public places to help the disabled integrate into society. At school my daughter sees people with similar or other problems. Many times she is useful to herself. She smiles with a certain understanding that bad as her condition is, there are many people like her and that many are even worse. That her case is not the worst gives her hope. She has regular medical check-up, most of it paid for by the state government. Western technology, medicine, and schools have given my daughter a better life.

In traditional Africa, sickle cell anaemia was given a mystical interpretation. Urhobo call the inflicted children *eda*. The affliction was a torment to ignorant mothers. The child that dies to be born again by the same mother! The child is never sated, the myth goes, despite the mother's grief. In many cases, innocent but old and ugly women were accused of witchcraft and, thus, of bewitching the victim family. There was (and still in many quarters is) no attempt to rationalize the disease of people carrying the trait or the disease in their genes increasing the chances of their offspring to get the disease. My mother lost many children after me. She complained of being bewitched. She made me and my brothers and sisters to be suspicious of so many people she did not like and felt would be happy to see her in sorrow. In hindsight, I can with certainty say that the infant children my mother lost died from complications associated with sickle cell disease.

My mother's family is also diabetic. There are a thousand myths woven around diabetes. I never knew of the Type 1 at home. The Type 2, the non-insulin dependent type was rare but there. This was due to obesity, which was also rare. People worked hard in the farm and this was their exercise. They ate natural foods. But rare as it was, there was no rational explanation. Who knew how many children might have died from complications of Type 1 diabetes or sickle cell anaemia? How many people, especially men, died of heart attack or stroke attributed to witchcraft that might have resulted from diabetes or hypertension?

I remember clearly when at about seven years old I went to visit my father. One of the most respected men in the village, who was described as huge, collapsed and died. There was no autopsy but traditional inquest that put the blame squarely on witches! I heard of other cases of seemingly healthy men in particular collapsing and dying. Nobody knew the stresses in their lives; nobody knew what they suffered from. In the cultural belief in the supernatural, almost every sickness or death was attributed to witchcraft.

Women accused of possessing witchcraft were sold into slavery in Ijoland. Similarly, men publicly accused of wizardry fled to distant lands to live without the stigma and shame associated with being a witch or a wizard. There used to be a time when the accused people would go to Uzerhe in Isoko to be proved innocent or guilty in a bizarre trial. At Uzerhe was a river and the accused were thrown into it – if they drowned, they were confirmed as witches by the priests; if they managed to swim out, they were hailed as innocent. They say somehow the innocent, whether they can swim or not, manage to get to land. But Uzerhe is a Catch-22. If you were accused, whatever your behaviour would be read negatively. If you walked fast, it would be said that Uzerhe had already possessed and snatched you away even before you got there! If you walked slowly, it would be said that Uzerhe had already killed you for your witchcraft before you even got there! Guilt was everywhere.

My mother tried many traditional medicines when sick to no avail until my wife persuaded her to go to hospital for a check-up. She obliged and went to Eku Baptist Hospital where she was diagnosed with Type 2 diabetes in 1989. With modern medicine and a lean diet, she has managed her diabetes well and looks good for her sixty-nine or so years. The West gives a second chance to Africa in many positive ways.

In Charlotte, North Carolina, I enjoy the conveniences and comfort (and discontent) of the West. I have phones at home and in the office, both with answering machines for a caller to leave a message if I am not there to pick up the phone or talking with somebody else at the time of the call. The phone at home has "call waiting," which means I can interrupt one call to answer an incoming call. I am yet to get the three-way system in which three different numbers could be connected to talk. I access my messages from anywhere, once I follow the instructions and use my code. You can't miss the instructions if you follow them correctly! I have a laptop at home and a Gateway 2000 computer in the office, both of which have Internet and e-mail facilities. In many of these services, you need a code or identification number so that your privacy will not be invaded. Despite all the precautions, I know the university authorities know my supposedly secret number and code and can access my messages. Big Brother is everywhere! There is also a fax in the office. In fact, in my office I am in touch with almost the whole accessible world. These are the staple comfort and conveniences of Western technology, an integral part of American life.

While in the United States, I am on cyberspace, the electronic superhighway. I am an explorer and can bump into somebody, for instance, in France or Australia. I can converse with friends daily without opening my mouth, without seeing them, without travelling anywhere other than to my office. I can hold a tryst with friends, even have an affair with a woman I have never seen, talked to, in cyberspace. This is definitely *oyibo* witchcraft. Everything is automatic, instant. Not only communication, but food also! There is instant coffee as there is instant tea. There will soon be instant love! The world is a global village, they say. It is not Oko-Igberhe. Nor is it Oko-Ibada, or Okurekpo. The global village is civilized jungle – New York, Chicago, Detroit, Los Angeles! The global village is littered with mines. So, beware!

Many of these facilities could be available at home. In fact, the woman living in my house in Effurun has cable television and her children are always glued to CNN International. The exhibitionist models are everywhere visible, more than half-naked, so over-made-up that they look not like the human beings they are but like aliens. Young men and women in Nigeria try to outbid each other dressing and behaving like MTV stars. They wear their designer caps turned round to look "cool." They wear torn jeans. And many girls are taking to smoking Virginia Slims. There is no end to the infection of the Western disease.

I fax messages to my Nigerian publishers and fellow writers. I remember the excitement with which Aig-Higo of Heinemann, Nigeria, felt when in two days we exchanged messages by fax five times. It was incredible, he felt. The white man's witchcraft can easily possess one. He was bewitched! There should be few e-mail facilities in Nigeria and one can say that many parts of Africa, except Zimbabwe and South Africa, have not even caught sight of the electronic superhighway of the twenty-first century.

I have always felt that my African people patented ways of sending messages and flying, which the European world people have stolen, appropriated, changed, and improved upon. We had the "talking" drum long before telegraph wires sprang up in Europe and the United States, long before Christopher Columbus was even born. With one drum, you can telegraph some news items across a large landmass. Growing up in Oko-Ibada and Okurekpo, I understand the language of my Agbon clan's drums. I know Urhobo drums. When the drum beats, I know whether it is a call for a gathering to discuss matters of importance or urgent issues, or a call for celebration of joy or sorrow. When somebody lost was found, it was an occasion for jubilation. When an old person "leaves this world for the next," we also celebrate his or her departure from this earthly plane for the spiritual.

We knew how to send messages instantly before the West started to develop them into a more efficient network to dominate others. The new witchcraft is not used to kill an individual you are envious of, but to keep down as living dead a race of people. I have always credited the European world people in their mass organizations, massive buildings, ships, aircraft, and others. They can also kill massively. With one bomb, the entire world could be wiped out. What a long way from Hiroshima and Nagasaki! The neutron bomb, the capitalist bomb, can even kill people and animals in an area and leave intact their belongings. I think the so-called developed nations of the West, especially the industrialized ones, have dropped a psychological neutron bomb on Africa. They are interested in such property as petroleum, diamonds, and gold. They do not care whether the people all starve to death under the burden of the IMF and the World Bank "conditionalities." Africans have been made to be eternal debtors of the West, and most of the so-called debts are very frivolous. Just numbers quoted to overwhelm the poor ones.

Let's come back to the issue of flying. Who first knew how to fly, apart from birds? Not the state of North Carolina that brags with "First in Flight." Our witches are said to fly in groundnut shells to distant places either to their covens or to bewitch somebody. They broke the sound barrier thousands of years before the Anglo-French Concorde jet started its transatlantic meteoric flight. The point is that the witches operated only at night. In a few cases, there were fatal accidents. If they were conveying poison to some place and the imminent victim had a strong soul, the witch could face difficulties and not be able to arrive. Then it suffered the fate of the proposed victim. They say they cannot cross the Atlantic Ocean to the United States, but they fly to England. Their actions are only known through confessions, done when they are very sick and afraid of dying. I have never seen anybody who says he or she is a witch. It is all hearsay and suspicions. Some medicine-men and women are said to have admitted to being wizards and witches respectively. I have a strong feeling that they want to intimidate their consultants and also show authority in the astral world to be believed.

I wrote a series of poems on European world indebtedness to Africa. These poems are in the collection titled *Daydream of Ants*.

The Script of Fate

They tattooed my skin
into a script of fate
needing no divination to read.
Those Grandmotherly lines
straight down the forehead
express wishes for prosperity.
The triple strokes on either cheek
racing left and right
weren't random scratches;
they meant life to readers.
Uli toned walls bright
with its black alphabet
in family signatures.
Hieroglyphs told full stories
of dynasties and their feats.
Tomes of clay, cotton, stone,
bronze and hardwood
bear on their powdered faces
weather-resistant lessons
lost to proud indifference.
It took the craft of born talents
to capture words and transform them
into a canvas of pictures.
And these literatures, handwritten,
remain unread and kept out
of libraries of knowledge
amidst a paper-choking world
of words, words, and words!

Scientists Without White Overalls

1
Chemist of unsung repute,
scientist of my birthplace,

you found the palm tree
one gift more than a thousand.

What stronger caustic acid
than the yield of ashes
of unseeded palm nut bunches;
what oil is thicker and purer
than the red one of ripe fruits?
And with a cauldron of mixtures
set to boil to a measured degree,
what foam left to cool and cake
gives a better wash?

2

They tagged my gin,
wholesale from palm wine,
the very drink of gods,
"ILLICIT"
because no market opened
for their flat brew.
Come to Okwagbe, sail
into Delta creeks
and the advanced science
of my own brew
mocks who-knows-what
bottled and sold dear
for London's Dry Gin
in supermarkets and bars!

Westerners have become the new witches in "*Discontent,*" *Daydream of Ants*:

I hear there are man-made rivers
for deserts to benefit from seas of abundance.
I wish the poor would be at the banquet.
I hear rain falls outside the sky
to grow shiploads of crossbred crops for export.
I wish the same craft promoted universal communion.

I hear rivers are run out of their courses
to stop deaths by drowning in frequent floods.
Imagine the damned plight of the weather-logged.

They predict the eclipse a century away,
monitor the pulse of the volcano to forewarn eruption,
shoot men into the moon to plant a proud flag.
A Duke friend announced to me
that his two-month pregnant wife
would deliver at 6 a.m. on July 5,
and that he had named the boy Jason.
Dream is no longer a sleeping experience
of fantasies; it's become a lifestyle.
Wizardry is performed in the full glare of the sun.

Some are discontented enough with God
as to mend the flawed earthencraft!

Africa and the West have complemented each other in more ways than they publicly acknowledge. Before Martin Bernal's *Black Athena*, I saw much of what is called Western has some Africanness. The Iberian Peninsula got much from the Moors and the Almoravides. Even the Greeks and Romans before them derived part of their civilization from Africa. In Mexico I saw that much of what is called Spanish is African from the adobe and on and on. The West's technological advancement and Africa's ethical advancement and humanity should complement the other. As I ask in "Voodoo Fever and Radiation Doses":

> How does a stethoscope
> repel voodoo fevers
> or herb-accompanied chants
> dispel radiation doses?

The love-hate relationship arises from the fact that much as Africa has gained from the relationship, the European world has gained even more, especially at the beginning. There is no longer good will. Things might have been better for us in more ways. European world people have confused military power (as a result of technological inhumanity) with superior culture. Even in the Christian Bible (and John Milton's

Paradise Lost), the Devil could beat God in a debate! Glamour and charm are not necessarily the essence. The untenable assumption of superiority on one side and the ability to exercise it has reduced Africa to what it is today. Like Walter Rodney, I know how Europe with its people worldwide has underdeveloped Africa.

V

Divine mentoring in poetry and its performance*

A people with a strong participatory artistic tradition as the *udje* dance songs of the Urhobo people are bound to have theory and practice of their popular poetic genre rooted in folkloric and mythic depths. To the Urhobo, poetry or song derives its *raison d'etre* from performance. In other words, a poem or song is not just imaginative use of language to express feelings or ideas in a special way. The poem's composition is half-done until it is performed publicly, a prior consideration that informs its technical and aesthetic form. This attendant process makes performance an inevitable and integral part of the poem. In the Urhobo tradition of literature, therefore, the poem is not completed until it is performed through singing out, often accompanied with drumming, clapping, and dancing on an appointed day in a public space that is open to all who want to listen and watch. The dancers often wear eye-catching costumes that give colour to the spectacle. It is this union of poetry and performance in the *udje* song tradition that the gods of *Aridon* and *Uhaghwa* come to play through human invocation a strong role in artistic creativity.

Gods and humans relate in the artistic realm of poetry and performance. There is a spiritual companionship that the poet and/or performer strike with the gods (Aridon and Uhaghwa). This relationship manifests in the physical world in the power of gods whose benevolence is proffered through service, devotion, and sacrifice. The muse figures, the tradition recognizes, possess or guard the artistic pool

---

* Charlotte, North Carolina. July, 2000.

of songs from which the poet derives his or her creative gift. The
mentoring gods imbibe the artist, poet and/or performer with the
necessary attributes to excel beyond the ordinary in the creative
enterprise. This takes the forms of *oruru*, zeal, passion, inspiration,
resourcefulness, vitality, and possession. The divine blessing of an
artist may just be creative and not material. In a song reflective of his
high artistic career which contrasts with his low social standing and
poverty, Majota of Uto quarter in Ekakpamre asks Uhaghwa:

> *Ukpe bi te re*
> *Otu r'Uhaghwa mi koko*
> *Nane ekpo obo ro obo-ole.*
> *Evwo te etiyi*
> *Obo-ole ovo enyerhare*
> *K'oye chere emu ria,*
> *Oma ye gbe vo we yo?*
> *Uhaghwa me vue we re.*

> (It's time again
> For singers and dancers to meet
> And go to the lead-singer's home.
> Should they get there
> And find the leader alone by the fire
> Preparing his own meal,
> Wouldn't you be ashamed?
> Uhaghwa, give thought to my plight.)

Majota, then in his fifties, had no wife, contrary to Urhobo tradition
of relatively early marriage. He is, thus, poor despite his poetic ability.
I will come back later to the role the gods play in the lives of the
devotee artists.

There are two sides to the song/poem that are correspondingly
enhanced by Aridon and Uhaghwa respectively. In the *udje* dance song
tradition, there are two key artists who bring to life the song: the *ororile*
(poet/composer) and the *obo-ile* or *oghwoghwile* (cantor/performer).
Though in some areas of the tradition, the term *obo-ile* is sometimes
used to denote the two principal actors in the process of *udje* dance
song actualization, the distinction of duties is clearly spelt out. The
poet, who is inspired, composes the song; then a sweet-voiced cantor
performs the song. The poet gathers the materials for and composes the

song, which he brings to his group's "workshop" for critiquing. There, colleagues "straighten" the song by paring it into a compact metaphoric quilt. Terms or images that have been used in other songs are removed so as to get a totally original poem.

After its acceptance as a finished poem/song, the group, which has played an editorial role, looks for a sweet-voiced singer to perform it. So, it is a form of audition for who can best present the poem for maximum effect for the pride of the group. In many instances, therefore, the poet is unknown to the public, only known to a coterie of the side's loyalists. The *obo-ile* or *oghwoghwile* presents the song in a live performance for the world to see, hear, enjoy, and judge. The *obo-ile*, two subordinate *ebo-ile*, male dancers, drummers, and female clappers dress in special costumes with long feathers, bells and rattles and perform the songs in a dance ensemble. It is the *obo-ile* who is usually an outgoing person who is acclaimed and praised. Of the great artists of the *udje* dance song tradition, the *ororile* and *obo-ile* or *oghwoghwile* are one and the same person. Oloya of Iwhrekan, Memerume of Edjophe, Okitiakpe of Ekakpamre, and Ope of Okwagbe in the Ughievwen polity of Urhobo are examples of the most talented poet-performers.

The arrangement of giving an individual's poem to somebody else to perform works well in the communal society in which the tradition of *udje* flourishes. The honour and glory of the quarter or town supersede an individual's egotistical desires for fame. Yet there have been instances when the poet had to prepare himself for the role of performer. According to Chief Jonathan Mrakpor, the man that Memerume handed over the laureateship of *udje* to in Edjophe, Memerume started as only a poet. His poetry was so good that the *obo-ile* or *oghwoghwile* bragged with the songs and gained all the fame. It was as a result of the anonymity of the poet in public places that he decided to also be a performer of his own songs. A smart person, he soon gained proficiency in performance, and he is generally regarded as next to Oloya, the greatest poet-performer in the *udje* poetic tradition.

The division of poet and performer in the oral tradition of a communal people is understandable. *Udje* is often described as "ofovwin," war, in which there are contesting parties for a winner. Since *udje* involves abusing another quarter or town with songs often exaggerating demeanors, there is intense rivalry and hostility. In order to surpass the rival side, practitioners seek the assistance of Aridon and Uhaghwa to excel in song composition and performance.

Let me further delineate the two stages of the *udje* dance song tradition. The poetry composition starts as an individual endeavour of foraging the imagination often in tranquillity for metaphors and rhythms that will result in the song/poem. There are testimonies of *irorile* and their coevals of poets humming to themselves parts or all of the songs they are composing on their way to work or in their workplaces such as farming, fishing, and hunting. Of course, among the non-literate people, the musicality of the poems, in the form of in-built rhythms with repetition, hiatus, and chiasmus, among other devices, helps the poet-practitioner to retain the song in his memory. The poet's work is, therefore, individually and privately done, apart from the "editorial" assistance in the "workshop." He derives his poetic strength from inspiration and the power of his imagination.

On the other hand, the *obo-ile* or *oghwoghwile* will broadcast the poem in a public performance. He practices singing the song and rehearses other aspects of the performance at night in the quarter's secret "workshop" in the bush, probably by the palm oil press. However, the ultimate in his career expectation is the festival day when he leads his group to perform before a crowd that will include strangers, members of the rival quarter or town, and the world at large. His objective is to enthral the audience through performance. His skills as leader, like the king in a chess game, have to be shown beyond his sonorous voice to include theatrical finesse, dexterity, and dance expertise and experience. In the tradition, while the *irorile* are usually older, the *ebo-ile* tend to be younger and more athletic to accommodate the theatrical demands of performance. Among the *irorile* who were also *ebo-ile*, Ekakpamre's Okitiakpe composed and performed to an age generally regarded as very old for a poet-singer-dancer; hence the rival Uto quarter abused him with songs. The versatile poet, in reply, composed the famous "Me vwe Odjelabo":

> Everyone will see for himself;
> If a child boasts to me,
> He will feel sorry for it.
> Everyone will see for himself;
> If a child boasts to me,
> He will feel sorry for it.
> If his tongue is sharper than mine,
> I know how to silence him:
> "That was before your time"

Will silence that child.
Uto's challenge has escalated
From revolver shootouts
To this aerial bombardment.
Uto is all bush.
Its people got wind of my gray hair
And are gleeful.
Since they are gloating around,
Have the old been driven from town?
The talk about my so-called age
Is more publicized than the first poll tax.
The fuss is unbelievable:
It is the head that grows grey hair;
It is not a dress I choose to put on.
This year we will see.
Gin may be tasty,
But palm wine makes it so.
When they challenged me,
They said they would stop at nothing;
Their words can never hurt me.
I am Odjelabo, the invincible.
Like Uvwiama, I am ageless.
Even when life is hard for a king,
He still has beads on his neck.
When it comes to dancing,
I am the peerless star;
First, like Eni among the gods.
Uto folks call me an old man;
But do they see age in a flying bird?
I have confidence in God,
And, besides, I am Uhaghwa's favourite.
It's good everyone sees for himself.

Okitiakpe says he may be old, but he is still very agile and is able to perform *udje* well. It is significant that he says, "I am Uhaghwa's favourite." This means that the god of songs and performance lavishes gifts on him.

While the tradition and its audience see poetry and performance as one process, still the two parts of this whole continue to be acknowledged as different. The poet serves Aridon, the god of memory and the muse; the performer also serves Aridon but more so Uhaghwa. Aridon requires an individual's service or sacrifice to have inspiration and also retentive memory. Thus, both poet and performer seek Aridon's virtues, one for poetic inspiration and fertile memory and the other for retentive memory in the arena of performance. With the hostility of rivals who could use diabolic means to "stop" the *obo-ile*'s voice, having Aridon charm becomes an absolute necessity. The "medicine" of Aridon is impressed upon an individual by a medicine man that puts together a small knotted bundle that includes a thread and a needle. There is the symbolic, rather semiotic, imagery of the thread leading to the source, the beginning. One can, thus, follow the thread to anywhere through divine assistance. The needle hits a fabric once and binds it! Both thread and needle are symbolically and mystically infused with the prerequisites of memory. In a ritual transfer of Aridon's power to the seeker, the medicine man uses the needle to stab the tongue nine times, the last carrying the Urhobo mystical invocation of *rhi rhi rhiri*. The medicine will have eternal effect on the person! Whether called *Era*, Aridon's role in assisting poets, composers, and performers is very clear.

On the other hand, the members of the troupe have both individual and public Uhaghwa, the "medicine" for attractive and flawless performance. The quarter or town procures the "medicine" for its performance. Usually, the "medicine" is prepared with scenting leaves of *ugboduma* plant, other leaves, herbs, and white chalk in a bowl from which, accompanied with a mystical chant, the liquid is sprinkled on singers and dancers in a ritual bath. A lamp is often placed beside the ritual bowl. A red parrot's or white eagle's feather or some other cherished feather is also part of this preparation. The medicine is then sprinkled onto the feather that the performer will wear in his hair or hat. If it is an individual's "Uhaghwa," the person strips and bathes with the water, often scrubbing the body with the herbs. As the bath is taken, there is the ritual chant of "Iye-e! Iye-e! Ekuvwie k'opha!" The chant invokes the applause given to a bride – in Urhoboland, the bride is taken to her husband amidst chants of praise and ululation. In the Ughievwen and Udu areas of Urhobo in which *udje* is prevalent, there are elaborate "*epha*" (bridal) ceremonies in which there is tumultuous applause of the brides. The medicine will transfer these charming qualities to the performer whom the audience will find enthralling. The performers, therefore, fully prepare themselves as individuals and as a group for their outing.

In many parts of Urhobo, especially the practitioners of *udje* dance songs, there are local names for Uhaghwa. In some areas, Uhaghwa is "Overe." In Iwhrekan, the god is called Oko. Owhawha people call the god "Diagbe." The local names are meant to domesticate the patron muse of artists with whom every performer wants to be in good standing. At the beginning of the performance, while announcing their readiness to perform as they "stroll" through the town, the troupe sings songs of Uhaghwa. Every group has its Uhaghwa songs.

Here are examples from different parts of the *udje* dance song tradition.

Ule Uhaghwa

E-he avwa rhire.
Ke mavo ame kare uwherhe?
Egha.
Mi ve omotete suko roko,
k'ovie ovwo ne ada kpo.
Owho ro uwevwin r'ighegbe
woma r'ikpokpo,
ke omevwen mi uwevwin r'isemeti?
Udu r'ohore re bru vwe-e.
Esa avwa rie vwe jovwo.
Edjalakpo no duvwu.
Idabolo rue ugen,
k'erherin agboro vwi yo.
Ehe, k'ahore vwi yo.
Okpako vue omo ota,
omi nyo;
obi nyo-o
oye ke ojefia.
Avwa rhi re.

Uhaghwa Song

We have come out.
How will sugar cane lack juice?
It never does.
If I compete with a child,
he will go home with tears.

Who lives in a glass house
boasts of throwing clubs,
what do I in a cement home care?
I have no fear going to any fight.
You already know my might.
Once the leopard catches a game, it's finished.
If you miss your way into my net,
you will be dried in a kitchen rack.
Let us fight it out.
When a senior tells a junior something,
he should listen;
should he not
that will be disrespect.
We have come out.)

Ule Uhaghwa R'ive

Uduvwu r'ovie
ovie de mue.
Akpo br'ise
mavo ivwori gher'urhie
yeya r'uvo.
Aphro ro jovwo.

Uduvwu r'ovie
ovie de mue.
Akpo br'ise
mavo ivwori gher'urhie
yeya r'uvo.
Aphro ro jovwo.

Diagbe, Diagbe;
Diagbe, Diagbe.

Eravwe r'awha de koko,
jama ke kpar'obo.
A-a do-o,
ehe he.

Uduvwu r'ovie

ovie de mue.
Akpo br'ise
mavo ivwori gher'urhie
yeya r'uvo.
Aphro ro jovwo.

Uduvwu r'ovie
ovie de mue.
Akpo br'ise
mavo ivwori gher'urhie
yeya r'uvo.
Aphro ro jovwo.

Uhaghwa Song: II

It is from the royal quarter
that a new king always emerges.
It is said
the creek cannot match a river
in withstanding drought.
That contest is futile.

It is from the royal quarter
that a new king always emerges.
It is said
the creek cannot match a river
in withstanding drought.
That contest is futile.

Diagbe, Diagbe;
Diagbe, Diagbe.
When animals gather,
the tortoise triumphs.
Greetings,
Greetings.

It is from the royal quarter
that a new king always emerges.
It is said
the creek cannot match a river

in withstanding drought.
That contest is futile.

It is from the royal quarter
that a new king always emerges.
It is said
the creek cannot match a river
in withstanding drought.
That contest is futile.)

The private and public domains of *udje* dance song tradition seek the assistance of the gods responsible for poetic inspiration, memory, and performance. They may be different but their favours are sought together in the sense that good memory and poetry enhance performance. Similarly, good performance necessarily involves a retentive memory, both of which enhance delivery of poetry. Sometimes Aridon and Uhaghwa are used interchangeably to mean the same principle or god of and "medicine" for inspiration, memory, and thrilling performance. The two artistic principles arise from the people's belief that the supernatural world has a bearing on human poetic creation and performance. The aesthetics of memory and performance demand a private composition that is actualized in a public performance.

Devotees of Aridon and especially of Uhaghwa believe that their gods have the power to protect them, hearken to their prayers, and make them to prosper in life. In a song to "Overe," a local name of Uhaghwa, a poet pleads:

My brother is sick,
And I am afraid.
Overe, I implore you;
Please, hear me.

Our women are sent to battle,
And the enemy is happy.
Uhaghwa, do you hear me?
My heart throbs with fear.
This is my brother,
My brother who helps me;
I trust him in every way.

There's dancing in the square
And I look out for my brother,
But do not see him;
He is very sick.
Overe, I beg you,
Beg you and beg you;
If my brother recovers,
We will all dance next time.

Uhaghwa is expected to fight on behalf of and for the interest of his artist-devotees, who are expected to offer the god sacrifice and service. In many Urhobo songs, especially *udje* dance songs, *ebo-ile* call on Uhaghwa to deflect from them any diabolic missiles that rival sides or victims of their songs might hurl at them. In an Otokutu song, the *obo-ile* says whoever attacks him will have to contend with the revenge of his mentor god, Uhaghwa. The poets and performers have total confidence in their Uhaghwa. A singer compares himself to a spirit: "Aziza mue ufi-i, oye egha Uhaghwa me" (The spirit cannot be caught by a trap; that Uhaghwa ensures). Oloya says: "Me vware Uhaghwa / me ke sue ole ri Tewhe" (I invoke Uhaghwa / before I begin to abuse Tewhe with songs). Sir Juju and Udjabor of Aladja call their Uhaghwa "Ovwile," the owner of songs. They state their trust of "Ovwile" as the opening formula of their songs, and then ask to be given "oruru," zeal to perform.

Almost all poets/singers in Urhobo have Uhaghwa songs, which are always passionate and highly poetic; these songs are tributes to their guardian and mentor god. In most cases, the singer or the group such as Johnson Adjah, Aribo Okpan, or Omokomoko Osokpa has a yearly festival during which he or she introduces the Uhaghwa song. The festival involves sacrifice of a cock or bull to the god of performance and muse to be ever more generous in inspiration and guardianship of the devotee.

I have written poems dedicated to Uhaghwa and Aridon. One example will suffice:

To Aridon

To the visionary of time-toned images
I return to gather my share.

To the memory god I return
to imbibe clarity
from his perennial stream

after revolutions of suns and moons.

Divine Sorcerer who captures
every day in its light and dark,
unwind your spool.

I will follow the sure lane of your thread
to cultivate correspondence.

I will follow to the farthest.

I want to rake your gift
from every nook and night.

I will be at the beach
to welcome the waves
you ride through

and be splashed with tales of blue.

I will scale the mountain
for your secret of elevation.

I want your measured rain
to wash off chronic dust
and to bring a record harvest.

To Aridon I must return.

In "The Fate of Vultures," I invoke Aridon to refresh the Nigerian national memory to track the loot of corrupt politicians.

A modern Urhobo writer, my songs/poems translate from an oral to a written tradition. These poems actualize themselves when read by others rather than when performed by me before an audience. But increasingly, I am trying to aim at performing the poems rather than merely reading them. A poem conceived to be performed engages poet and audience in a different way from the one meant to be merely read.

To prepare myself to be better equipped for performance, I took lessons from the great *Opiri* music exponent, Ogute Otan. For four weeks in the summer of 1998 I visited him at his Okumagba Layout home in Warri to dialogue with him on poetic creation and performance. By then, he composed his oral poems with the assistance of a cassette player, which he played back and forth to strengthen his breath spaces, metaphors, and rhythms. I saw firsthand how modern technology enhanced an oral tradition.

Ogute Otan taught me how to beat the drum while singing to enhance the rhythm and liveliness of a poetic performance. In "Drum Suite," I conceived a poem to be accompanied by drumming, a percussive rhythm that "ki kiki / koko gi kogi" underscores. Here is the oral poem in a written medium:

Drum Suite

The elbow has found room in the crowd,
let it rest and give the body desired peace

*koko gi ko gi
ki kiki
koko gi ko gi*

the mouth spits out the body's fire,
let fresh winds blow inside

*koko gi ko gi
ki kiki
koko gi ko gi*

the road of the pathfinder has become a river,
a boat already waits for the crossing

*koko gi ko gi
ki kiki
koko gi ko gi*

two travellers bring their roads to one,

let them cavort at the crossroads

koko gi ko gi
ki kiki
koko gi ko gi

the full moon relieves the night of its sadness,
the ram nudges his spouse with horns

koko gi ko gi
ki kiki
koko gi ko gi

two fugitives have caught one another by the arm,
let them rest on the other's reciprocity

koko gi ko gi
ki kiki
koko gi ko gi

That's my story of deep water,
only the divers know its depth

koko gi ko gi
ki kiki
koko gi ko gi
ki kiki
koko gi ko gi

What are the implications of invoking Aridon and Uhaghwa to the modern African writer? There is divine or spiritual sanction to oppose all types of evil and social transgressions. Political corruption and all forms of inhumanity that go against the national ethos have to be exposed so as to be eliminated. Many African writers see this didactic function as part of their role in society. Some may be subtler than others; but, generally, there is the attempt to lead the society into a course that will ensure peace, stability, and prosperity.

The African writer's career, therefore, needs courage as both the *ororile* and *obo-ile* in traditional *udje*. He or she must have the courage to damn it for the sake of telling the truth that will save the society and the values it holds dear. As traditional practitioners of the *udje* poetic genre contend with victims of their abuse who make "medicines" to hurt them, so do modern writers in Africa have to contend with corrupt leaders, dictators, and others that transgress positive norms. Traditional artists derive their courage from the divine mentors of Aridon and Uhaghwa. They are fearless and believe that the muse-gods have sent them on errands and they must deliver their messages however unpalatable to the powerful ones of their societies. The modern writer may or may not believe in the efficacy of traditional gods or "medicines," but still have on their side the invisible angels of truth on whose behalf they fearlessly march. The writer should not be afraid to propose a vision, however bitter it may taste, if he or she knows that it will lead to the salvation of the entire the society or its marginalized segment.

There are risks involved in being an artist, and that has led many to jail and even execution. Dennis Brutus, Wole Soyinka, and Ngugi wa Thiongo have gone to jail or been exiled for their outspoken ideas. In recent times, Jack Mapanje was jailed for railing against the late Malawian tyrant, Kamuzu Banda. In Nigeria, Ken Saro-Wiwa was executed for his defense of environmental and minority rights of the Niger Delta peoples. So the risks are there as a traditional artist and a modern artist. Aware of the risks, the artist still remains loyal to the muse to whom he or she does not lie. The muse of many African writers today may not be Aridon or Uhaghwa, but the principles the two gods represent remain the same. For most, the muse is now transformed into the common people, the weak, the poor, the neglected, and the disadvantaged of society.

Being an artist or writer today in Africa is more than chasing the beauty of form or aesthetic concerns alone. The spiritual (moral or ethical) fortification of society falls into the writer's responsibility. In traditional societies, there are annual festivals when there is spiritual cleansing – there is the invitation of spirits in a communion at the end of which there are sacrifices of atonement for the ills and misfortunes of the previous year. There is public acknowledgment of infringements because societal values are public property whose preservation should be every individual's concern. It is during such festivals in the "kingdom of songs" that *udje* dance songs are performed in honor of Aridon and Uhaghwa.

The writer today in Africa, very aware of the socio-political and economic problems that beset the society, has to use his or her talent to steer everybody like a good shepherd to the idyllic conditions of his or her vision. Serving the society positively as *udje* artists did and still do is as important a concern as the entertainment aspect of the writing. Nothing is "extra-literary" in a literature that helps in the preservation of a people's cherished values.

The culture that nourished me has its imprints on me and on my artistic creation. The spiritual dimension of gods or "medicines" of Aridon and Uhaghwa has bearing on my tapping from great depths the poetic and performance resources that my people, especially through the *udje* dance songs tradition, have exercised for hundreds of years till now. *Udje* dance songs may be giving way to the so-called "Urhobo disco," made popular by both Johnson Adjan and Okpan Aribo, whose songs still carry the divine and human mediation that continues to be manifested in poetry and performance to achieve artistic excellence. Traditions transform themselves over time and continue to manifest, with the assistance of new tools and media, the same effects that gave birth to them. The spiritual side of poetry provided by Aridon and Uhaghwa still persists and should transfuse the written lines of modern poetry with fresh blood and vitality.

VI

Self, myth, and historical consciousness: an African writer's reflection*

With the birth of a new twenty-first century, there are calls for predictions about what direction Nigerian or African literature would take. Faced with such requests more than twice, I started to reflect on the direction of any national or cultural literature. It is my contention that the direction of any literature has more to do with the prevailing conditions of the writer's time and his or her individual response to them, brought about by the personal life of the writer. Some scholars may argue that a people's literature can consciously move toward set goals, but I feel that a writer or group of writers could break out and form the trend, which is not dictated but blazed by one or a few and followed by others.

Time in place appears to me to be the greatest conditioner of a writer's work. Of course, Bhaktin and others have written on geotope, on the importance of place and time. But I am looking at the course of an individual's or a group's literature from personal experience. When Osip Mandelstam wrote *On the Noise of Time*, he was apparently talking of the place of history. The individual writer is conditioned by the prevailing sociological, political, and economic conditions of the time in the place of birth or residence. The place we are born into already has a mythical and historical reality. The time has bearing on the writer's individual condition and he or she has to respond to happenings around him or her. Is it a place of tolerance or not, is there freedom or not, justice or not, and the other socio-cultural factors that

---
* Charlotte, December 2000.

make a place a handmaiden of history? The more negative forces around such as corruption, dictatorship, oppression, and marginalization, the more the keen sensibility of the writer will be aroused to challenge them for positive virtues. Self is inevitably tied to history.

The writer can express self as autobiography. This may be objective or subjective, depending on the form the writer chooses. Writing a memoir is about the self in an objective way. On the other hand, expressing experiences in a poem is presenting the self in a subjective way. By the time the poet uses metaphors and other figures to describe personal experiences, he or she is being subjective; at least what he/she writes has subjective connotations.

The personal self whether objective or subjective can also be the human self that the writer shares with others. The writer is a human being who has to confront the vagaries and necessities of existence. Thus, he or she is like every other human being that is "I" and "We," which re-enact the individual and the collective. For the African writer who is raised in a culture replete with rites of passage, this is very significant. There are times the writer has to contend with the singular self and at other times with the plural/collective self. As will be explained later, the self is embedded in the group psyche that fosters myths.

At a creative level, self is often a mask that a highly talented writer like William Shakespeare can use to multiple advantages. This is what John Keats calls "Negative Capability," the ability of the artist to assume the personality or voice of a fictional character. I have tried to assume a personality which, I believe, is not mine to say something. When one assumes what one is not in real life, one imbibes empathy. The self appears in the form of the persona used by poet. The ability to assume different voices or personalities tells something about the person.

In some instances, the writer creates personal myths to express himself. He quarries for metaphors, symbols, and other figures to describe the assumed role. In African literature, especially in poetry, writers have assumed the personae of myth-maker, town-crier, pilgrim, wanderer, quester, warrior, troubadour, scribe, and others. Okigbo saw himself as a creator of myths, as also a prophet who warns with his iron bell.

The self is responsive to experiences, which are brought about by the intersection of time and place. The self can be a lone country, but is serviced by the outside, the domain of history and myth.

Time, therefore, seems to be the immediate conditioner of self and human experiences, more so in Africa with its history of slave trade, colonialism, neo-colonialism, and post-independence experiences. The writer has to be conscious of the prevailing conditions of the time and position himself on the side of humanity, justice, fairness, and other positive values to advance the march of humanity to a higher state of consciousness. It is important to note that one should go against the prevailing conditions if they are against humanity. It is from this acknowledgment of the place of history that the role of the poet as a prophet derives. Christopher Okigbo, Lenrie Peters, and Wole Soyinka, among others, want the reader to see through the façade of currency. The writer should denounce a government that does not respond to the basic needs of its people. Also opponents of a government should be condemned if their vision is exclusionary, whether based on ethnic, class, regional, religious, or other narrow considerations. The primary good should be for the benefit of the generality of the people.

Historical memory and consciousness affect a people. Jews and Nigeria's Niger Delta people come to mind. Niger River Delta people are not an ethnic group but people whose area has through its economic resources given the people a sense of cohesion. As history brings social, economic, political and other changes to individuals and groups (nations), so does our world-view change with specific individual or group experience. So, Nigerians as a people have passed different stages of history, which affect them as individuals and as Nigerians. The writer needs not share in either the justified historical optimism or a simplistic schematic optimism of Lukacs, but should be aware of the times so as to project a vision that enriches humanism for *now* and the future. The writer cannot escape history even as he or she sees the future as a challenge. As sociologists like Omafume Onoge and Joseph Obi see it, literature is a testimonial or visionary exploration. In either case, history drives it, since it engenders sensibilities, which are sometimes produced by contradictions of time. I do not feel that the writer should accept a determinist concept of history, because that will limit the effort to change things and enhance humanism. Even in such a concept, the writer should still engage in struggles, which may be futile but ennobling. Tragedy itself could still enhance humanity. A materialist concept of history leaves more room for the writer to project optimism. But I do not need to accept the views that history is materialist or determinist, linear or circular, to know that history directs human experiences. Of course, the reverse view that humans make history could be argued. In our time, in Africa in particular, a revolutionary reading of history seems more apt because of its relevance.

Let me examine the concept of myth and then place self before it and history. Myth is a communal property, the people's folklore. It is there for the individual to share with others of the same heritage. The "others" could be an ethnic group, a state or region, nation, continent/race, and also humanity. Thus, myth could derive from a circle that is sometimes narrow and at other times wide. This range registers the "self" as an individual and as a human being in a universal context.

Proverbs, for instance, are mythical. In oral tradition, their origins can barely be ascertained, but they have gained such currency that they become acceptable formulae in sagely speech or general oratorical traditions. As the Urhobo people say, the footprints of an elephant are not difficult to tell. The repertory of a people's beliefs, world-view, and philosophy becomes the domain of myth.

Traditional African oral culture has myths for every possible thing and phenomenon. Myths can be said to be politically correct explanations that elders give to inquisitive children to explain why things are what they are. For example, when a child, my grandmother told me why the sky is so high, why men and women cannot do without each other and yet are always quarrelling, why humans die, and many other things. A myth tries to explain a phenomenon. Many myths that explain why things are what they are can be said to be etiological tales. Why does the pig/hog always look down, why does the hen take water in drops, and so forth?

Myths form a part of a tradition, a generally public domain. Like African oral tradition, there are many myths in ancient Roman and Greek cultures. Ovid's *Metamorphoses* is a mythical opus. Myths are built around humans, plants and animals of a people. There is a story about a local lake near Ughelli where a bride who used to come there to bathe with her maids looked back and was transformed into a tree!

Myths are related to history in the sense that they are continually being created. As long as there are groups, communities, nations and races, fresh myths emerge. Myths and history are handmaidens. When Europeans came to West Africa at the beginning of the twentieth century, they brought the mammy water myth, something like a transformation of the mermaid and sirens in a different environment. Originating from India, the myth travelled to Europe (Germany) before coming to the western coast of Africa. This light-complexioned rather slim and attractive lady is half-human and half-fish. In some paintings, she wears a python as a necklace. Once the Jebba Bridge across the River Niger in Nigeria was built, myths sprang up like mushrooms. The master-artist Bruce Onobrakpeya recalls how so many workers were dying while the bridge was under construction. This was traced to a water spirit who felt violated by humans. Subsequently, the spirit was tricked by a European into a bottle and corked. From then on, there were no more deaths of workers.

I have been at seminars and other forums in which some scholars took myth to be arcane practices and customs. Myths are ideas attached to concrete happenings, living things and humans, or phenomena. Myths are not necessarily static, but like culture always evolving and dynamic according to the people's socio-cultural evolution. Many myths transform in the tradition of a people. I have observed how the Olokun myth transformed to Mammy Water and the two water-related myths have basically merged into one in many parts of southern Nigeria. Wealth and beauty derive from water or the sea, according to this very myth. My Urhobo people as fishermen and women made a living of what the waters give out; hence their world-view. However, the coming of Europeans with luxury goods to seaports reinforced this concept of wealth coming from the sea. The Urhobo say, "Olokun, bie emu rhe vwe" (Olokun, row your boat of prosperity to me).

Writers have used myths for as long as literature has been an integral part of their lives. Writers as individuals in societies often deploy myths in their writings to conjure up images for self-expression. The argument is not whether one uses myth or not, but to what use myth can be put in literary composition, oral or written. Like everything else, it can be used positively or negatively. It is only a vehicle or medium of expression. The writer who is progressive embraces the dynamic essence of myth, which he or she uses as a revolutionary transforming tool or even weapon. On the opposite side of the argument will be the writer who embraces the static antiquated notion of myth.

I believe that Wole Soyinka in his poetry embraces the revolutionary ethos by way of myth in both "Idanre" and *Ogun Abibiman*. In "Idanre," the "septuple god," Ogun, becomes a

Prometheus figure who defies personal comfort and convenience to bring humans transformational tools to build what has led to the present civilization. In *Ogun Abibiman*, the poet summons the same god as well as Shaka in a revolutionary endeavour to smash the injustices of apartheid in then South Africa.

My drama colleagues including Iyorchie Hagher and Dauda Musa have contested Soyinka's use of myth. Where I, the poet, see revolution, they see a reactionary posture. I agree with them that Soyinka's use of myth in his plays is problematic. *Death and the King's Horseman* is a case in point. There, many critics see Soyinka as indirectly defending the practice of ritual suicide. But it seems to me that the Nigerian dramatist is only using a cultural practice to make a more fundamental point in tragedy. Of course, history (in this case the colonial administration) impacts on traditional culture. The play also speaks of the relativity of cultural practices; hence the comparative presentation of Yoruba and English ways. In any case, from Soyinka's example, one writer in different genres could in the praxis of deploying myths be seen as having antithetical results. This example confirms my thesis that myth could be dynamic or static, revolutionary or reactionary, indeed positive or negative. It all depends on the use to which myth is put.

Let me add that though generally myths derive from a folk tradition of a group, individual artists are known to create private/personal myths. Here the self and myth meet and sometimes merge. The renowned Nigerian poet, Christopher Okigbo, created myths in *Heavensgate*, *Limits*, and *Path of Thunder* to express the nature and role of the poet amidst contemporary happenings. Self, myth and historical consciousness harmonize in poetry of the highest lyrical quality in Okigbo. In his last poems, the poet is a town-crier alerting his people to what is happening and forewarns about the dire consequences of their actions:

> The elephant, tetrarch of the jungle:
> With a wave of the hand
> He could pull four trees to the ground;
> His four mortar legs pounded the earth:
> Wherever they treaded,
> The grass was forbidden to be there.
>
> Alas! the elephant has fallen –

Hurrah for thunder –

But already the hunters are talking about pumpkins:
If they share the meat let them remember thunder.

The eye that looks down will surely see the nose;
The finger that fits should be used to pick the nose.

The then military coup has set a dangerous precedent whose perils the poet warns the Nigerian public and readers against. In Okigbo's poetry, myth is used to convey a mask, a persona, through which the poet comments philosophically on historical happenings and human existence.

I see myth in its revolutionary use as a necessary creative metaphor of the writer, especially the poet who is activist and intent on bringing about positive changes to the society. A myth can serve as a means of resistance and liberation. I have in recent times looked at Urhobo/Edo myths and attempted to relate them to contemporary happenings. In September 1999, I prefaced the "Home Truths" section of *In the Kingdom of Songs* thus:

> For many years I have been studying my native Urhobo and Edo folklores for images, symbols, and icons of transformation, metamorphosis, and change that can be related to the African condition amidst contemporary happenings, conditions, and phenomena. My interest in traditional and contemporary African art has sharpened this pursuit. It is my desire to be rooted in African culture and still be able to explore issues and problems from a wider philosophical perspective.
>
> Among aspects of transformation that I think of as I write these poems are mythic heroes, especially healers, transformed into features of the landscape, including trees, and which became the focus of religious worship. I also think of themes of death and renewal as in the planting of yams which "die" before they grow. I have been reflecting on the mudfish's practice of transcending natural and spiritual boundaries in its ability to stay in dried-up streams as if dead and to come back with the new rains. There is spiritual transformation in the ability of healers and others to harness the power and life force

of the forest for the benefit of the people, especially their use of herbs from the forest to control ailments. There is, as observed by Susan Vogel, a natural connection of material, mythic, spiritual, and cosmological phenomena in the complex symbolic links between certain species of animals – birds, reptiles, fish – and the power to transform.

I find it necessary to observe the present from a historical perspective, metaphorically captured in myth, and to use the lessons philosophically absorbed in the process for a better future. Thus, the healers and other mythic heroes serve as counterpoints to many of the rulers of present-day Africa. Extolling the selflessness and service of humans "transformed" into demi-gods should serve as a weapon of resistance against dictatorship, selfishness, and greed which currently plague much of Africa. The exploration of transformational myths should also serve as a metaphorical invitation to Africans to commit themselves to those virtues that their own cultures once nurtured. This will involve exorcising the evil of corruption, repression, and greed. African societies used to have healers and other mystical figures that exercised power for the benefit of the community. Thus, irrespective of the very form of government adopted in a country like Nigeria, the collective psyche of the leadership and people has first to change before there can be any meaningful governance. A people should learn from their past mistakes to avoid falling into future pitfalls.

The lessons of myth for any individual or group are many and can help to direct towards development.

Let me not forget to mention "Archetypes." These are myths that reverberate in many cultures and seem to have a worldwide presence. The very essence of human existence bringing together physical and spiritual, secular and religious pre-occupations set the backdrop of myth. Life and death breed myths. The search for salvation in an afterlife perpetuates myth.

The contemporary writer or critic should not embrace a narrow view of myth and feel that it should be discarded. It is a tool that can be renewed, transformed to stronger personal use to give poetry the vitality and depth it always will need.

As I have always emphasized, the writer is not an "air plant," and so is rooted in time and place. The self is subjected to the geotope, as it responds to what goes on around. The individual writes in a context, which appears conditioned by history and traditions that feed the creative spring. Self, myth, and historical consciousness give context and specificity to the writer.

VII

Nigerian literature in the twenty-first century: what direction?*

Modern Nigerian literature has gone a very long way from the 1950s to the present. We should take a moment to celebrate and pay tribute to those – living or dead – who brought this about. Amos Tutuola, Christopher Okigbo, Chinua Achebe, Wole Soyinka, John Pepper Clark, Gabriel Okara, Flora Nwapa, Zulu Sofola, and Ola Rotimi, among others. Nigeria undoubtedly contributed to making West Africa to flourish with literary creations in the late 1950s and the 1960s, when East Africa was still a literary wilderness! Nigerians have won awards such as the Nobel Prize, the Commonwealth Literature/Poetry Prize, the Booker Prize, the All-Africa Christopher Okigbo Poetry/Literature Prize, the Noma Prize, and have been candidates for many more awards. Ours is a great inheritance that we need to celebrate. At the same time that we celebrate it, we should make a deliberate effort to build upon what has been handed down to us at the beginning of the twenty-first century that future generations will be most proud of.

What do we want for Nigerian literature that we have to work towards? We expect the highest quality of literary artistic production that will reflect our culture and project visions relevant to Nigerian cherished ethos. We need more productivity at the individual and national levels. Nigerian literature should embrace writings from different parts of the country and there should be from us a concerted effort to promote creative writing in areas that have up to now not been quite productive. It is imperative for Nigerian literature to reflect the totality of the national experience. For this reason, I believe that there

---

* Keynote Address at the Association of Nigerian Authors' Convention in Jos, November 14-19, 2000.

should be promotion of more writing in the northern part of our country. Indeed, there is excellent writing from Algeria, Egypt and Morocco, Muslim states whose religious and cultural practices are similar to those of Muslim Northern Nigerian. There is no reason why the predominantly Muslim North should not make its contribution to Nigerian literature. In addition, more women writers should be encouraged to write and publish for gender balance – there is much the women writers could do to give Nigerian literature more breadth and depth. There should be more writing in Nigerian languages, not only to complement what is written in English but also to reach Nigerians who only understand those languages. Furthermore, a concerted effort must be made to publish and publicize more of the younger writers so as to bridge the widening generation gap between the older and younger writers. Also, we should look toward a participatory literature of more readers as writers reach more people.

Before I begin to plan, prophesy, or second-guess what direction Nigerian literature should take in the twenty-first century, I seek to indulge you in a philosophical reflection over the following: conscious and unconscious influences on planning, accidents, and the climate of the time. This also involves what we have control over and what we do not. When one talks of direction, is it only forward, or could it be sideways, backwards, upward, and downward? Direction has to do with time and space, what the Russian Bakhtin calls "chronotope." Should a nation's literature aim at a specific direction or struggle towards the aesthetic and cultural ideals the people envision, and in the process bring about changes? Is Ngugi wa Thiongo right to say that "Change is...the eternal theme in history" (*Moving the Centre*, p. 96)? Should history not be left alone to struggle towards its own "centre"?

I am not going to enter the debate as to whether history is materialist or determinist, whether it is linear or circular. In any case, memory of the past and realization of the present will prepare one to anticipate the future. Memory of the past is very important, hence I started by asking for a celebration of the past and present, and paying tribute to those writers, who blazed the literary trail for us to follow. Time and space will always provide the context of Nigerian writing. There are new frontiers ahead and the challenges have to be met.

In the lives of individuals and nations/groups, there are conscious and unconscious happenings – people plan and prepare to implement, but there are historical factors, including accidents of history, that condition our reality reflected in drama, fiction, and poetry. So the direction of our history will, to a large extent, condition our literature. The extent to which historical memory and consciousness affect the individual will set the direction of Nigerian literature in the twenty-first century. Thus, self, collective identity of nationhood, and how they play in the circumstances of the time will direct Nigerian literature. Also the relevance of ideas is closely tied to the socio-political and economic conditions of a nation, which again affect the lives of the people and literature. What I am driving at is that whatever direction we as writers may wish to take will follow the flow of Nigerian history and conditions. We can aspire towards certain goals, but we do not know how those goals when affected by historical realities will manifest in literary ideas, form, techniques and overall aesthetics and tradition. The writer's individual condition has bearing on the time – is it a place of tolerance or not, is there freedom or not, justice or not, and the other socio-cultural factors that make a place a handmaiden of history? The more negative forces around such as corruption, dictatorship, oppression, and marginalization, the more the keen sensibility of the writer will be aroused to challenge them for positive virtues. As long as Nigeria is not stable, not democratic, and not fair, the writer cannot defy history, but will only reflect that reality and propose a counter positive vision.

While relevance will always be a watchword, there is nobody, I believe, who can divine the future with exactitude. We can only speculate from our short-sighted but real present and, while projecting our ideals ahead, be ready for uncertainties of the future. You have put on me the responsibilities of a seer, which I am not. How do you project the direction of Nigerian literature in the context, for instance, of a New World Order or globalization, which controls us in such ways as publishing, distribution of books, publicity, readership, and earnings from writing? Publishers have their editorial policies, which affect the types of manuscripts they eventually publish. With many Nigerian writers seeking to publish outside, how will they be influenced by the traditions of writing that foreign editors propose to them?

The direction of a national literature depends not only on the writers but also on sociological factors, the condition of the people and time, and economic, political, and other realities.

Nigerian writers are one family with a common tradition. In a family, there are regulars and deviants, odd ones, parasites, protesters, humorists, serious-minded, and even freaks. All are members of one family but acquire a variety of personalities. There should be no attempt to hedge everyone into one pigeonhole. In variety and diversity are vitality and strength. Our writing must be free, unshackled by any dogma, uncensored by writers, critics, government, or socio-cultural prudes. It is freedom that will lead to experimentation in form and technique and proposition of fresh visions for society.

We must avoid inbreeding, which results in weakness and poor health. Though the apprentice needs a master, he or she should follow whomever he or she chooses, but shed influences in time not to be seen as a clone. Clones are monotonous. Writers, especially young ones, should feel free to choose what to read and be bold in experimentation. If you notice soldier ants, they are seemingly moving in opposing directions but are indeed moving forward towards a goal. What direction should Nigerian literature take? I will say, not one direction. We must not lose touch of our identity (culture and unique problems), but should not close ourselves to other traditions of writing. Nigerian writing in the twenty-first century should take many directions, but each direction must be purposeful.

There are core values of, for instance, honesty, sincerity, selflessness, generosity, and kindness, that will lead society at all times towards humanistic goals of justice and fairness for all. While time and place will condition us individually and collectively, consciously and unconsciously, writers must not only be reactive to what is happening around and in the world, but also be proactive. Each generation carries its responsibilities in society, and it is necessary to fight against negative qualities and to project positive alternative virtues.

The best education for the Nigerian writer for the future is within – zeal, self-confidence, and dedication. The writer must enjoy writing for its own sake first as actualization of inner feelings before seeing it as an avenue for financial gain or promotion in the academy. Every writer must establish a close bond with writing. A writer must be dedicated, persistent and committed, and these qualities will show in the works over the years. With dedication, it takes ten to eighteen years from the time they first started writing for most writers to get established. And that's where patience counts. The Nigerian writer has to learn to be professional, and can accomplish this by subscribing to or reading creative magazines.

Talking of Nigerian writers' source of strength being within, let us not forget our respective heritage of orature. What the Spanish Federico Garcia Lorca said of gypsy songs is true of Nigerian oral tradition – "the artistic treasure of an entire race is on the road to oblivion...Old men are taking to the grave priceless treasures of past generations" (*Poem of the Deep Song*, ii-iii). It is every Nigerian writer's responsibility to save by at least modernizing a dying tradition. Our literature will become more vibrant if we research into indigenous oratures and acquire those forms and techniques rather than read antiquated foreign literary traditions that have no relevance to our experience and aesthetics.

There are many indigenous forms on which to model. What could be more poetic than Idoma *Aliekun*, Mernyang *Se-chan*, Tiv *Anzaakaa*, Urhobo *Udje*, and Yoruba *Ijala*, *Oriki*, and *Rara*, for example? Our own fabulous tales had to travel across the Atlantic to the so-called New World to become magical realism in Latin America. Now when a Nigerian writer writes in the style of his or her people that even Amos Tutuola used, critics see him or her as being influenced by Garcia Marquez! Drama, fiction, and poetry have more than enough models in indigenous cultures to reinforce Nigerian literature of the future.

Nigerian writers should not respond to foreign critics who denigrate their works by writing to fulfil their canon's demands. I have personal experience of a Nigerian critic concurring with a British critic's comments on a Nigerian literary work on the basis that the Nigerian writer does not obey British poetic tradition. Literature is a cultural production, and each culture has its values and aesthetic concerns. In fact, Nigerian writers should subvert Western epistemology meant to reduce Africa's humanity.

Nigerian authors should avoid the opportunism of jumping to write on what Western critics look for and do not see in our writings. There have been Nigerian authors who have played extreme negativism and pessimism about Nigeria to please outsiders. Others have jumped to write on gays and lesbians or female circumcision because they form part of the discourse on Africa in Western academies. We should integrate into our works the Nigerian reality and fiction, pessimism and hope, but let it be from within, not from a desire to please foreign readers and critics to hear strange things about us.

Let me take one by one certain Nigerian realities and factors that will willy-nilly affect the direction of Nigerian literature in the course of the twenty-first century.

Nigerian writers have to be very mindful of the people for whom they write and whose values they articulate. The anticipated audience affects the language/diction of the work. In the general Nigerian context, a writer could be very creative and simple. A writer who writes what his or her people cannot understand will be irrelevant to their daily and perennial struggles. This does not mean that the writer should not challenge the minds of his or her readers. I believe Nigerian writers should exploit the resources of Pidgin English and indigenous languages to reach a wider audience.

This could lead to writers reading and performing their works. If writers envisage performance as one of their literary goals, the consideration will affect the form, content and diction of their works. With more readings, production of plays, and performance of, especially, poetry and short stories, there will be a lot of excitement and more literary production. One fairly certain direction that Nigerian literature should take this century is that of performance to establish a wonderful rapport between artists and their audiences.

Nigerian writers should not be shy in writing in their indigenous languages to develop their literatures and cultures. Imagine reading or performing poems in your language to small family groups, and then moving to larger street-side and open theatre audiences. Currently, there is a lot of performance of literature in South Africa and Zimbabwe, and we could learn from them to enliven our national literature.

Teachers and critics have a special relationship with writers and can affect the direction of a national literature. One may not agree with Chinweizu's tone and style, but I am convinced that he helped to mold the poetic attitude of a generation from the mid-1970s through the 1980s with his *Towards the Decolonization of African Literature* and caustic criticism of the early poetry of the Nigerian "euro-modernist poets." Critics and teachers are more relevant in today's society of the New World Order. Teachers can interest students in Nigerian literature by using modern pedagogical tools such as video, CD-ROM, and the Internet. Nigerian writers should make use of the new technology and post their works on the Internet for wider readership and availability to teachers and students. This means that writers should try to have home pages that will draw attention to their works. While Tijan Sallah and I were assembling poems for *The New African Poetry: An Anthology*, we read many South African poems posted in the Internet and selected some poems from there for inclusion in the anthology.

Critics and writers traditionally have a symbiotic relationship. Critics study writers' works and point out strengths and weaknesses that might help improve future writings. A lesson from the criticism of Nigerian literature so far is the emphasis placed on form over content by one generation and content over form by another. Nigerian literature, especially the poetry, should balance content with form.

However, in recent times of literary theories generated feverishly in Western academies for promotion, tenure, or stardom, critics tend to act in a way as if they do not care about creative texts. Our teachers and critics should not pander to these foreign theorists by using their theories to evaluate Nigerian, albeit African, literary works. We should not give the impression to younger writers that their models are outside and not among us because African literary works may fall out of sink with rules of western literature, just as theirs with ours. Imagine putting a square peg in a round hole! We can learn about theories but must be wary of their use. Theorists tend to focus on fiction and avoid close readings of texts, but our teachers and critics should read texts and not leave out poetry and drama, major African literary genres.

The publishing culture has suffered terribly because of the collapse of the national economy as a result of political corruption and mismanagement of resources. There is currently in Nigeria barely any standard commercial publisher of literature. The multinational publishers have severed cooperation with their local counterparts – Heinemann, Longman, and Macmillan, among others. Of the small and other presses, they foresee no profit in publishing literature books even though people hunger for them. They publish biographies and memoirs of military and political officials and launch them to make money. While they have a right to publish these ego-boosting books, they should take literature seriously. It is true that constant closures of schools and universities adversely affect them, but they can still make profit if they publish standard works.

Nigerian publishers should do a professional job in having high quality production, which involves good packaging of books. With very little effort and a little care, Nigerian publishers can do well with paper quality, book covers, and proofreading. They should know that writers are Nigeria's ambassadors to the world. Our books have to be available to outsiders and be seen as well produced for Nigerian writers to compete on equal terms with others. As a juror for an international literary prize, I recommended a very talented Nigerian writer most of whose works have been published in Nigeria. Though I talked about the quality of his writings, my fellow jurors were not impressed by the quality of the production of his books compared with the well-packaged books of other candidates. The point is that the publishers will do themselves and Nigerian writers much good if they go for high quality publication. If the Nigerian author won the Neustadt Prize, it should not have been only $40,000 in his pocket, but it should have put him on a faster lane to the Nobel!

I find it ironically more acceptable for established writers to do self-publishing than young writers who may need it for exposure. Professional publishing with its editors helps to eliminate problems of language, organization, and overall content of a literary work. Sidetracking editors and paying for a work to be printed is fraught with dangers. There are many works in print that are sloppy, full of mistakes, and not worth showing anybody or being read as texts. While it is important to get published, young writers should be patient not to rush to print their works. If they must, they should seek editorial assistance from experienced writers or university teachers to go through the works.

I suggest that the Association of Nigerian Authors should seek private and corporate funds to publish several works every year. The Association could start with works that win prizes and later increase to two of drama, fiction, and poetry respectively every year. There are so many art-loving rich people and companies that will contribute towards this endeavour. And, of course, the Ministry of Culture should be approached to contribute towards this project. ANA should set up an editorial board that will screen and edit works before publication.

Whatever direction Nigerian literature will take in this century depends on the vitality and dedication of now young writers and others yet to be born. I advise that the young should not be intimidated by the old. They should challenge the tradition – discard what is not relevant and absorb what will complement our values – without losing sense of direction. ANA should put in place through its local associations a system of mentoring young writers. That will be an investment that could yield high dividends in future.

Women writers' horizons should be expanded so that they can have more space and time to devote to writing. Husbands, parents, and relations of female writers need to show support by not seeing writing as a form of rebellion. In fact, writing makes one more humane. Let the women writers not only have a room of their own, but also we should free them from some chores to give them time to write. No matter how talented a person might be, he or she must have the time to exercise that talent – very many talents never realize their potentials, and many women are in that category. With conscious effort in society, we can help our female writers to be more productive in the exercise of their talents. The society should be less critical of women expressing themselves so that they can avoid self-censorship that besets many women writers in Nigeria. Nigerian literature will definitely take an upward swing for a gender inclusive humanity if our women writers are supported.

Having said this, I will advise Nigerian women writers to be dedicated to their writing and strive for the best quality possible. They should work hard and be judged on the basis of the quality of their work and not just on gender. I consider it demeaning for a Nigerian female writer to be seen only in, for instance, women's-only anthologies.

Nigeria has very few avenues of recognizing and appreciating her talents. Nigerians do not need to wait for outsiders (usually Europeans and Americans) to recognize their writers with awards, fellowships, job offers, and other honours before they do so. Soyinka won the Nobel Prize before his own country belatedly awarded him the Order of the Niger. At least one of our young writers has received an honorary doctorate degree from a western university and I am yet to hear of a Nigerian university that has honoured any of our post-Soyinka-Achebe generation writers. We should look at ourselves and give honour to those who have achieved it.

Today I have come from outside to meet with my fellow Nigerian writers. There are Nigerian writers today living in Botswana, Britain, Canada, Germany, Ireland, Lesotho, South Africa, and the United States of America. There could be others I have omitted. This will no doubt have its fallout on Nigerian literature, as there will be the temptation for writers outside to be influenced by the traditions of the places where they write and publish. This will spell more hybridity that writers who have become Nigerian by naturalization or association have already started. I think of the energy that Karen Aribisala and Kanchana Ugbabe have brought to Nigerian literature.

Let those abroad and those within work together, reinforce each other, just as South Africans did during the apartheid era. Those abroad with perhaps better resources should assist those at home in whatever way they can. There should be no hostility or accusation of betrayal, but they should see themselves as branches of one family tree.

Government, private individuals, and corporations should promote competitions to generate writing. If writers have income for time without work, they will be more productive. ANA should think of building or raising money to build artists' colonies and encourage the rich and corporations to set up endowments for such colonies where writers can withdraw to and write without interruption.

Nigeria needs a National Endowment for the Arts to give fellowships to writers, starting with about five a year and to grow to ten or more with about ₦600,000 per fellow a year.

The state, in a non-partisan way, can help to generate interest in writing. One of the ways the state can do this is by appointing a poet laureate for a term of two years. The works of whoever is appointed will be promoted, and this will help in developing all of Nigerian literature. Perhaps, the person should be called the National Griot/Griotte.

Finally, while writers as individuals and as a group should arm themselves for the writing career with its highs and lows, I prescribe no single direction. All directions are there, but we should not go backwards. Let us invest in the future of Nigerian writing for it to achieve greater heights. And while doing this, let us be true to ourselves, to our heritage, and to our tradition.

Upon all I have said, the emergence of literary giants and geniuses will shape the direction that Nigerian literature will take in the twenty-first century. Let me end by quoting our Wole Soyinka: "Unsuspected founts of social energy may erupt beneath our feet with profound devastating insights and organizing genius." This is the direction I hope for Nigerian literature in the twenty-first century – the path of genius, whichever way takes us there.

VIII

Whose English? The African writer and the language issue*

One of the assumptions in the English-speaking world is that once you come from Africa, you must be more fluent in a native language than in English. There is also the assumption that just because somebody is from England, the United States of America, Canada, Australia, or New Zealand, that person's English must be good or correct. Of course, from my experience of studying and teaching in the West, these assumptions have little or nothing to do with reality. Many Africans almost start speaking English and their mother tongues at the same time, and because the State encourages education in English, proficiency in English soon exceeds that in the native language in many cases. For many of us who teach English or Literature in the United States, it easily dawns on us that one may speak only one's native language (in this case English) and not be good at it in writing, especially when it comes to being grammatically correct. I have observed American senators, academics, and so-called educated people speak or write English in a very sloppy manner.

So, it is with a measure of exasperation that the African writer in English has to respond to European world people or Americans when asked: "What language do you write in?" That is, sometimes, after they already know that, like me, you took a master's degree in creative writing and a doctorate in English. To be fair to some of those who ask such questions, in a normal world one should write in one's native language. In that ideal situation, I should be writing in Urhobo, my Nigerian mother tongue, and not in English. But the world, as will be explained later, is not an ideal configuration. There are powerful states

---

* Rockefeller Centre for Scholars and Artists, Bellagio, Italy. August 5-6, 2001

and there are weak states. Besides, colonization has affected non-Western peoples, especially in Africa, in rather permanent ways.

I once argued with a professor of comparative literature who strongly felt good poetry (it depends on his definition!) could not come from small (native) languages and also that somebody whose mother tongue was not English or any of the major European languages could write great literature. That was at a seminar on "Mother Tongue, Other Tongue" at the University of Iowa, Iowa City, in 1984. Many of us participants were in the International Writing Program. I argued, supported by the late Ivar Ivask, then editor of the prestigious *World Literature Today*, that good poetry has to do with a writer's or rather artist's imaginative intensity and perception rather than the language *per se*. Of course, the comparative literature professor either had not heard of or deliberately ignored *The Mwindo Epic*, *Sundiata*, *izibongo* chants, *ijala* and *oriki*, and *udje* dance songs all composed in native African languages by talented griots. However, by 1986 when Wole Soyinka of Nigeria won the Nobel Prize for Literature, the professor conceded that after all Soyinka wrote in English! He had moved grounds a bit, though reluctantly.

By the early 1980s began a trend of fine writers emerging not in the metropolitan language centres but in the peripheries – the former colonies or minority groups within the English-speaking nations. There could be many factors responsible for this. In Africa, the euphoria of political independence and the subsequent disappointment with the political leaders had their parts to play in the creative outburst of the time. The winning of the Nobel Prize for Literature by Derek Walcott of the Caribbean, the Black American Toni Morrison, the South African Nadine Godimer, and the Irish Seamus Heaney confirm the full blooming of the trend in the anglophone world.

So, one would expect by the new century/millennium that native English speakers should have made peace with the phenomenon and understood why the trend would continue to gain ground; but things have not been so. The assumptions continue to be blurted out by so-called scholars and intellectuals. I felt disappointed when I read in the *National Geographic* that Saul Bellow of all people derided African literature. Only recently, an Englishman said that the language of non-native speakers of English is *terribly* limited. Since he did not qualify his statement on who the "non-native speakers" were, I disagreed with his view and told him that, in fact, those of us creative writers from outside the metropolis of English have a natural advantage in the use of the language over the "native speakers." This, I explained, was because we *have* a very rich vocabulary that our individual and national experiences together with the particular environments have combined with the regular English he spoke. Many words of West African English are not in the *Oxford Dictionary*! Some like *kwashiorkor, garri, iroko,* and *fufu* are getting in with time. I will later on in the essay expatiate on this point together with varieties of English such as Pidgin.

Writing poetry in English, I take the challenges of both the right and the validity of the non-native speaker of English to write creatively as personal. It smacks to me of needless arrogance and ignorance of the capabilities of "others." There is the inference that literature written outside the metropolis is inferior to that of the native speakers of English, a point I believe is far from the truth and, in fact, in contemporary times the other way around. As the debate has not abated, I feel the issue needs to be revisited and put in its proper perspective of today. This raises the question, "Whose English is being debated in writing?" I will use my personal experience of writing in English and teaching English/literature in English in the United States to attempt to answer the question and make personal comments on my writing in English.

I do not want to belabour the point, but it still needs reiteration that once there was European colonization of Africa from the nineteenth century onward at a level not earlier experienced in history, the language of the colonizers became property of the colonies. This is the implication of things not being ideal in the world that I referred to earlier. Whether it was the so-called *indirect rule* of British colonizers, the *assimilation* of the French, or *assimilado* of the Portuguese, the European colonizer in Africa, by force of arms as authority, imposed his language on the peoples he brought together for his economic advantages into one "modern state." By fiat of the pen at Berlin (November 1884-February 1885), the European "powers" ratified their "spheres of influence" as nations. These new countries were almost in all cases created out of heterogeneous groups. Nigeria has more than two hundred indigenous languages. English remains the official language till today, a century after the first series of protectorates were established.

While it is true that most of my age-mates started learning English from elementary school, we were already speaking languages into which colonial English had already made a lot of inroads. This was what the cultural thrust of colonization was all about at the time. In fact, among my Urhobo people, so many foreign words had already entered the lexicon. Portuguese words started it: *kujere* (spoon), *osete* (plate), *ughojo* (clock/watch), *oro* (gold), *meje* (table), *sabato* (shoes), *isama* (salmon), and so on. English words came in later but became more accentuated with the process of colonization. There were words, which were just Urhoboized because there were no native equivalents of such foreign words. *Imoto* became the Urhobo word for motor/car/truck; *gareji* for "garage" (bus stop); *kolta* for coal tar; *kurumani* for crewman; and *itaba* for tobacco.

It was in the area of fashion and modern technology that new words mainly entered the local languages. The colonial administrators wore a khaki hat called "Cork" which in Urhobo became "koku." I have a friend whose father's praise-name is "Koku," to which he responds "It completes a gentleman's dressing!" A Western Nigerian colonial administrator like Bourdillion gave his name to the hat he wore. The type of shoe he wore became fashionable as "zagzone," a neologism in Urhobo language.

Thus, even before one entered school with English teachers or with teachers of English, the foreign language was already subtly making inroads into the imagination of the young colonized African. Before I went to school, Roman Catholic reverend fathers were already playing an active role in the life of the village. You did not need to be a Christian or a church-goer to call the Irish Catholic priests "ifada," fathers, and where they worshipped with their converts "ishoshi," church. Many words like "baptism" and "marriage" which could not easily be translated retained their English nomenclatures in Urhobo. Also there were *itisha* (teacher), *ikuku* (cook), *iboyi* (boy), and *iledi* (lady). Many boys were called *Boyi* and girls *Iledi*. In fact, one of my two close boyhood friends was named Iboyi and the other Godiwini (Godwin). My senior half-sister is called Iledi. How voracious for English my people were! So, there was a lot of baggage of English with many of us in the early 1950s before we entered elementary schools, most of which were run by Catholic or Anglican Church missionaries who were English-speaking Irish or English men respectively. Even when still non-literate, English was already indirectly rooted in the language and life of the people.

It was mandatory that modern education be given in English, even if you had the rare opportunity, as I had, to spend the first three years to partly learn to read and write Urhobo. You had to go to "isukuru" (school) every day except Saturday, Sunday and "holide" (holidays). You had to buy your "exercise book," either "2A"or "2B." No child of my age or Elementary Class I was deceived that the ultimate education was not in English. *The Queen's Primer* was a required text, and, in fact, most of us bought it and repeated "I Tee, It" long before the book was due to be used. For the next several years in the primary school we would learn to read and write English.

The colonizers came to Africa for economic gain and wanted to maximize their economic exploitation. The more peaceful the colonies were, the easier they made profit and ran the affairs of the country through intermediaries of the Queen (or King) in England. Thus, to run a smooth colonial administration, they needed to train a group of Africans to assist them in their colonial project. They needed interpreters, clerks, house helps, and so forth. Teaching English to the subjects, rather than learning the local language, became part of the colonial enterprise. The process of deracination that they contrived would make the subject Africans more dedicated to the colonial cause. This they did with some zeal because it was in their interest for a class of native speakers of English to be created as soon as possible to ensure smooth and profitable administration of the colonies.

In the colonial enterprise, the missionary and the colonizer worked together. The colonizer, in many instances, left education of the "natives" in the hands of so-called "God's men." We as kids were not fooled that the missionary and the colonial administrator were different. They were all "oyibos," always consulting and in each other's company. The more English you spoke, the more you gained their favour. Since authority lay with the colonial administration, you got better hearing with English. In court, people who should be found guilty and convicted won cases because they told lies in English. Oppressors who spoke English cast themselves as victims and had the wrong people punished.

So-called English names such as Moses, Peter, Joseph, and others were given to pupils as soon as they entered school and coerced to be baptized. It was assumed that the local birth-names were not good enough for God at baptism and so some European saint's name or obscure Old Testament name was adopted to be a true convert. On my first day at school, despite protests from me that I am Emoghware, I was forcibly given the name Moses! While African names make meaning, especially based on circumstances of the child's birth, the foreign names were culturally irrelevant. However, the native's proficiency in spoken and written English was beneficial to the missionary who brought the Bible to evangelize and to the colonizer for the reasons aforementioned.

We did some study of English in the elementary school, as would be expected of children in any language anywhere. But it was a good beginning. I knew older people like my uncles who became proficient in English after completing only Standard School and could write and read letters. By secondary school, English had become the sole medium of instruction and communication between teachers and students and among students. On my first day at St. George's Grammar School, Obinomba, we were slammed with Rules and Regulations meant to be enforced vigorously. The first rule was: "No speaking of Vernacular. Anybody caught speaking Vernacular would be given ten strokes of the cane. Repeated violation will lead to suspension for a month." This was read to us as a riot act the very evening that the new students, all boarders, arrived! The second rule, which really was a corollary of the first, banned the speaking of Pidgin English. So, there I was with my cousin, Samuel Onosigho, from the same home because my maternal grandmother raised me, and we could not speak Urhobo together. There were Frederick Siakpere, Joseph Oderhowho, Fidelis Overo, Solomon Ugbogure, and others from the same Okpara, but we could speak to each other neither Urhobo nor Pidgin English that was the lingua franca of the Niger Delta region. I could not learn to speak the Ukwani dialect of the Igbo language that was spoken in the area! I had to speak English all the time at school. So, for the whole five years in secondary school, we were stuck with English. The missionary educational ploy or policy worked in the sense that gradually all of us saw ourselves as "Georgians" speaking English. My first language of talking with people from outside my ethnic group was English! English, by fate of colonialism, became our language, not just only English people's.

English was taught rigorously in the secondary schools of our youth. There were almost daily composition assignments. My principal at Obinomba, Father Cunningham, taught us English and did it as if it were a mortal sin to make a grammatical mistake. Up till now, I can't tell whether the reverend father was as interested in our spiritual salvation as in our mastering grammatically correct English! After all, we were in a "grammar school" and we had to be "grammarians"! The syllabus for the West African School Certificate Examination in the early to mid 1960s focused on composition, clause analysis, and other aspects of grammar. No candidate passed the General Certificate of

Education Examination conducted by the University of Oxford or the West African School Certificate Examination conducted by Cambridge University without passing English. In hindsight, St. George's rigour helped us to be always out for grammatically correct English whether spoken in our own accents or written.

Many of us in secondary schools and later in Higher School Certificate or Advanced GCE programs started writing through Press Clubs, Debating Societies, and other societies that encouraged writing or speaking English. We wrote poems or short essays and stapled them to a designated board for other students and teachers to read at Federal Government College, Warri. Exercising proficiency in English is a deep-rooted tradition for many non-native speakers of the language.

By the time of entry into the university, the student, whether English major, minor, or not, was expected to have a high standard of English proficiency in reading and writing to study effectively any discipline. Nobody was admitted into the regular university programs without a credit in English language. How could you become a lawyer, the Registrar's Office reasoned, without good English to read and comprehend tomes of books? How could you become a medical doctor without being able to read the literature of the field? English had become the language of successful professionals.

Those of us who chose to read English/Literature had to effectively study the language and the literature. With Professor Harold Whitehall and Professor Ayo Banjo to guide us on the language side of our studies and many toying with linguistics, we had ample experience of the English language. Of course, in literature, we read what could be read of English literature, including Geoffrey Chaucer's *Canterbury Tales* in its original and selections of William Shakespeare's tragedies, comedies and histories. We were lucky that we read African literature too and had firsthand experience of how the earlier generation of Africans such as Chinua Achebe, J.P.Clark, Christopher Okigbo, and Wole Soyinka, among others, had successfully used the English language in their writings. How proud to read Soyinka's "Telephone Conversation" in which the Nigerian poet makes fun of a native and racist English landlady! Okigbo's incantatory lines were mesmerizing. Our British lecturers included the versatile Scottish Dr. McVeigh, Mr. Corner, Dr. Young, and Miss Poullin. In weekly essays and assignments and the final "long essay" the language drilling was perfected. At exams, there was the effortless writing of long answers to questions, as if the length of the answers meant better grasp of the issues involved in the question. Many students were fond of calling for more answer sheets either to impress the lecturer or intimidate fellow students. In any case, a large measure of ease with the language promoted this. I will in my American teaching find the generality of students scared of essay types of answers in examinations. Most would answer a question with a word, not even a complete sentence! These students are native speakers of English!

For many in my generation at the University of Ibadan creative writing was encouraged in the many student and university magazines then flourishing. The *Beacon* was a major one. Departments also had their own journals. In addition to these magazines and journals that published student writings, we had a Creative Writer's Club that made us creative kindred spirits. Many of our teachers encouraged us in the club. So, to me, having a degree in English was not merely studying English, but had more that would make me a poet today from the encouragement of Professor Whitehall, the magazines, and the student writers' club.

It should have been unnecessary to give this chronology of the place of English in the African writer's life and his time. But because of the assumptions mentioned at the beginning, the explanations become inevitable. English is the language of communication for the educated ones in Nigeria, as in other former colonies of Britain. English is the official language of Nigeria, not Hausa, Igbo, or Yoruba. It is the language with which Nigerians of different ethnic groups communicate. It has become an act of fate but nonetheless a reality of our lives till now and perhaps will still be for a long time.

What are the implications of the long association with English, which has become a normal language for an African writer like me? If the English people wanted for all times to have their language to themselves without any varieties, they would not have taken part in colonialism. But they did and gained economically from the colonies such as Gold Coast, Nigeria, and Kenya. If they wanted their native language to remain untouched by historical circumstances, they would have desisted from shipping away to other worlds their outcasts, rebels, and others. But they did, and today have the pleasure of a small country giving the world a universal language. English, whether American or British, is at the bottom the same language. With so many Englishes out there, geographical, historical, and cultural circumstances have moulded different varieties.

Despite the attempt to suppress African indigenous languages in schools, most writers speak their mother tongues effectively and use the resources of those languages to enrich English. Each African language has its folklore, which its native speaker now writing or speaking English exploits to the fullest. Achebe and Soyinka have effectively accomplished this interface in their writings.

As I write poems in English, I use images and symbols, which derive from my Niger Delta environment. The fauna and flora of the area become metaphors that give a distinctive colour to the work. When, for instance, I use the tortoise as a symbol of greed, the hyena of tyranny, and the vulture of a despicable character, the British and American native speakers may not easily comprehend the mythic associations. Many proverbs from African languages lace English with oratorical devices, which are fresh and exciting. African writers, carrying a wealth of native folklore, are some of the major users of proverbs in their literary works. I have not read a novel by an Englishman or American that has as many proverbs as in Achebe's *Things Fall Apart* or *The Arrow of God*.

The constant reference to the *iroko* tree and the eagle in my poems carries folkloric connotations that may not be easily decoded by readers outside of the Niger Delta, albeit Nigerian, culture. The *iroko* tree is the tallest and biggest tree in the rain forest area. It is a symbol of strength, invincibility, and greatness, since the strongest of storms cannot uproot it. The tree is also imbued with mystical power, as its bark is used for traditional medicines.

I see myself as having an advantage writing poetry in English because I am bringing into the language freshness and vitality that the native speaker, to whom the language has become blasé, cannot bring to it. What is an English person going to write that will not be traceable to their great predecessors – Shakespeare, Milton, Dryden, Wordsworth, and others? The language on its own, as used in England, can barely generate freshness or vitality. Many Irish writers of English are able to infuse Gaelic or Celtic culture into the language. The examples of James Joyce, Samuel Beckett, and Seamus Heaney are illustrative of how another culture could be used to shock English into unexpected vitality. Soyinka's plays in the early 1960s did as much with their Yoruba subtexts. These examples confirm that English, as it is today, would be a worn-out language without the subtexts of other cultures to enliven it. For poetry in particular, the subtext gives another level of meaning to the work. Without it, the poetry is flat.

Poetry raids the frontiers of language. The non-native speaker of English can range freely and imaginatively, drawing into the artistic work images and icons that a different culture has established. The topicality of other places without English customs, the invention of new words in places unimagined by the forebears of the language, and new developments worldwide all contribute positively to a vibrant literature in English. New connotations and collocations will always stretch and enrich the English language. Some American writers who draw on an additional culture such as Irish Americans, Jewish Americans, and Black Americans must be aware of the need to infuse mainstream English with something different to enhance the vitality of their creative language. A poet like Gary Snyder had to borrow from Oriental philosophies to give a distinctive colour to his poetry.

A further advantage of non-native speakers of English writing poetry in English is in the variety of forms available to them. Many of us African writers have a multiplicity of traditional rhythms that enrich our poems. Traditional forms of praise, abuse, dirge, and others have their rhythms, which we borrow. Even when the diction is English, the form may be African. I tend to read my poems aloud as I write and test how well a specific piece obeys traditional African rhythmic form rather than the English iambic pentameter. I feel challenged in exploiting the words of English to resonate in a tonal African language's rhythmic pattern. Since music spices poetry, the additional blending of African and English rhythmic patterns, when properly used, can only enhance the passion of a poem.

As a principle, I write my poems and other creative works in West African English and my scholarly essays and books in American English. West African English is a local variant of British English. The syntactical structure, spelling, punctuation, and other grammatical and technical features are slightly different from those of American English. I am able to switch from one to the other as appropriate for my writing. Writing poems with a primary African audience, I choose to write in the English of my people. However, since most of the journals in my field are in the United States and drawing on my graduate experience, I write critical essays in American English. Many times I have to ignore the Microsoft Word spelling guide, which is programmed on American English system. Being familiar with three or more varieties of English definitely gives an advantage in using the language creatively.

While I have dealt with my personal experiences, many other writers, especially of my generation, have similar experiences of a different kind. I believe Niyi Osundare, Chimalum Nwankwo, Tijan M. Sallah, and Syl Cheney-Coker, among many others, have had similar experiences in West Africa and in the United States as I have recounted. Some of the assumptions I have referred to must have affected African writers in the United States, Canada, or Britain. Though I have taught creative writing (poetry) in two colleges, it is not easy for good African writers to be hired to teach creative writing. It took Cheney-Coker quite some years to get a regular teaching job. While I feel Osundare is the leading poet in New Orleans, at least in his university, he was for a long time excluded from the Creative Writing Program!

In a recent incident, a Chinese American composer asked a retired Oxford professor why his accent was different from his wife's. He had to explain that he had no accent, but that his wife came from another part of England. In the group there was an Englishman living in the United States, whose accent was recognizably neither American nor British. The question was most revealing as everybody now has an "accent." The American has an accent outside America; the African has an accent outside Africa; the Briton has an accent outside Britain! There are now many Englishes. Whose English do I write? It is ours, not by choice but by fate and nonetheless ours to use creatively.

IX

Expanding the curriculum in American schools: why include African literature?*

American schools have increasingly embraced multiculturalism, cross-culturalism, and diversity in recent years, no doubt to remedy a former lack of openness, breadth, and depth in the school curriculum. The former curriculum focused almost entirely on the Anglo-American literary heritage and failed to reflect the diversity that is the reality of the American experience. After all, America is a melting pot of peoples of different cultural and ethnic backgrounds, including Blacks, Hispanics and Native Americans. The largest minority group is made up of African-Americans, who have a direct connection with Africa, from where their forebears were taken as slaves over a period of three centuries. The new development of inclusion in the school curriculum is welcome, as cultures grow even stronger when they exhibit multiplicity of textures. It is in light of the trend in expanding school curriculum that I argue for the inclusion of African literature.

Literature, a cultural production, is a multidisciplinary field in the sense that it involves anthropology, economics, history, music, religion, sociology, and other disciplines. African literature, as exemplified by such works as Chinua Achebe's *Things Fall Apart* and Alan Paton's *Cry the Beloved Country*, has become the window through which outsiders view Africans. African literature reflects the African condition in economic, political, and socio-cultural matters. Books such as Festus Iyayi's *Violence*, Achebe's *A Man of the People*, and Ngugi wa Thiong'o's *Devil on the Cross* illustrate the respective conditions of

---

* Presented at a Seminar on Diversity and the School Curriculum at the National Afro-American Museum and Cultural Centre, Wilberforce, Ohio, November 9-10, 2000.

African societies in different places at different times. In addition to teaching African literature as a specific subject or part of literature, therefore, I recommend that teachers of African anthropology/culture, history, philosophy, politics, religion, and sociology also use African literary texts. Works of African literature serve as literature as well as tools for the teaching of the human and worthwhile aspects of the continent of Africa and its people.

African literature, a product of African culture, is directly related to African-American culture and literature. Residues of African culture abound in African-American culture, especially in the areas of myth and folklore. Henry Louis Gates, in his *The Signifying Monkey*, sees the African trickster motif (the Yoruba variant in particular) mediated upon by the American environment in the works of Zora Neale Hurston, Ishmael Reed, and Alice Walker. My first experience of reading Hurston's *Their Eyes Were Watching God* was of feeling a subtext of African language use. John W. Robert's *From Trickster to Badman: The Black Folk Hero in Slavery and Freedom* also treats the trickster motif in African-American culture, which originates from Africa. Furthermore, Joseph E. Holloway has edited *Africanisms in American Culture*, which deals, among others, with folklore and other artistic expressions of African-Americans that are traceable to Africa.

Exposing American students to African literature will therefore paradoxically make them understand their own literature the better. By knowing the African experience in literature, they will be able to figure out the subtexts of American, especially African-American, literary texts that are consciously or unconsciously influenced by African culture. This could help them to highlight the connection with and disconnection from African-American literature. Since literature is a cultural production, there are features of the African oral tradition that continue to remotely affect African-American literature. In other words, understanding African literature will reinforce understanding of American literature in the same manner that knowledge of British literature helps to understand the tradition from which Anglo-American literature grew. Experience of African literature, oral and written, will give depth of approach to African-American literature, a major component of American literature. It is significant that Toni Morrison in her *Tar Baby* uses a common traditional African myth/tale that has many variants.

African literature provides a comparative perspective on American literature. For this reason, it will broaden and deepen understanding of not only American literature but also literature generally. From an artistic perspective, African literature exhibits features that are different from American literature. Its aesthetic considerations are different. Traditionally, arts (including the verbal ones) have their functionality and value as major aesthetic criteria. African literature generally is didactic and focuses on the content (not necessarily at the expense of form) for its meaning to be clearly articulated. The writers tend to be activists, as they involve themselves in politics and social affairs in varying degrees. In their poems, novels and plays writers assail the corruption, tyranny, and nepotism of their leaders and governments. It is for this activism in the socio-political life of their states that African writers are thrown into jail, and a military dictator executed the renowned Nigerian writer Ken Saro-Wiwa.

This literature is different from the art for art's sake phenomenon that is generally common nowadays in the West. Chinua Achebe and many African writers have drawn attention to the western writers or critics' complaint that the African writer is too serious and too earnest. It is in the African literary tradition to be serious and earnest; more so as the writers tend to reflect the reality of their people. The condition of things in Africa is such that the writer cannot ignore the plight of the people for whom and on behalf of whom he or she writes and still be relevant. Achebe, for instance, explains why he wrote *Things Fall Apart* and some of his other novels. He sees the writer as a teacher. He shows in his first novel that "Africans did not hear of culture for the first time from Europeans, that they had a philosophy of great depth and value, they had poetry, and above all they had dignity." He also says that he wants to use his novels, based on Africa's past, to inform and educate Africans that their past had not been one great night from which the Europeans woke them. This double-audience aim of Achebe to speak to European people and to his fellow Africans is part of the audience-conscious feature of African literature, first manifested in the oral tradition and then passed on to writing. Some other African writers have seen themselves as their people's prophets, seers, shepherds, and warriors.

What are the implications of these artistic roles for Americans? Through exposure to African literature, American students will have a broader view of literature and culture. Many American critics would see politics as "extra-literary," but not so to African artists. To the African writer, the socio-economic and political problems of his or her people are valid materials for poetry, drama and fiction. African literature will stretch and expand the concept of literature, as Americans generally know it. African literary aesthetics in particular will demonstrate that what readers expect from literature may depend upon their cultural conditioning and not one specific universal feature. This is multiculturalism that globalization makes even more relevant and urgent today than ever before – the ability to know so much about others to reinforce oneself. In fact, knowing about the "other" makes one look more critically at the "same." African literary aesthetics, therefore, can only help to broaden and deepen the concept of literature as known to Americans.

I want to add that there was a debate up to the 1950s as to whether literature can be oral and whether African oral narratives in the forms of tales, myths, legends and epics and poetry in the forms of songs, chants, proverbs and others were literature. Even Ruth Finnegan, who had worked on African oral traditions, was reluctant in accepting the apparent "contradiction" that oral works could be literature. By the 1960s, even the cynics had accepted that literature could be oral, noting that before they were written down the first epics of the West were oral creations. Today, orature is a legitimate component of literature.

It is very significant that African oral literature involves performance. In traditional African literature, there is barely a generic separation of poetry, drama, and fiction. Understanding African oral literature will help to break down the departmentalization of literature for something integrative – a multi-genre.

One cannot argue against the claim that there are values in other cultures that can be beneficial to American youths, and that African oral literature is, potentially, a great source of moral and ethical instruction. The sense of community and selflessness espoused in African folk tales, as in that of the tortoise in Achebe's *Things Fall Apart*, will counter both the radical individualism and the "me first" attitude that pervade the current generation of American youths.

At least in the African-American segment of the society, the idea of "it takes a village to raise a child" challenges the sense of responsibility of every adult in a community. In an age in which peddlers of drugs are glamorized because of their wealth, responsible adults will put the youths on the right moral path. The selflessness demanded of a communal society does help to refocus the minds of youths on not just immediate material pursuits and things but on character building for future careers and social consciousness. Besides, African orature could be a counterpoint to television violence and sex that the young see as real life that should be tried out.

African literature relates to African people and society, hence its unique "aesthetic modes" and "cultural and social structures." Its "essential force," as Abiola Irele puts it, is "its reference to the historical and experiential" (11). The following are some of the cultural traits of modern African literature, even when written in European languages:

i) **Utilitarian function of African literature**. Literature, in the African tradition, entertains and educates. In the African context, there is almost no art for art's sake.

ii) **Ethical and moral nature of African civilization**. As elders in orature used folk tales to instruct, so do modern writers take on the role of the conscience of their societies. Writers generally condemn the negative aspects of society such as corruption, tyranny, and greed, among others. The didactic role of African literature persists in more subtle ways than in the oral tradition.

iii) **Social cohesion**. There appears in many African literary works no single individual as protagonist because of the communal lifestyle of the people. To the African, the following dictum is quintessential: "I am, because we are; and since we are, therefore I am" (Mbiti 108-109). The ideal of social solidarity is expressed and emphasized (Kunene xvi). Wole Soyinka's *The Interpreters*, Ngugi's *Petals of Blood*, and Achebe's *Anthills of the Savannah* are novels in which the protagonist is diffused into several characters. Generally, there seems to be not much emphasis on one character. Rather, the community is portrayed as much of a character as other humans interacting in the society. In Achebe's *Things Fall Apart* Umuofia is clearly delineated as much as Okonkwo, an Umuofia man.

iv) **African village life** is "filled with belief in . . . mystical power" (Mbiti 197). Elechi Amadi's *The Concubine* and Zulu Sofola's *Wedlock of the Gods* are examples of works that treat the mystical and supernatural in African life. Divinities proliferate in African literary works, as in Achebe's and Soyinka's writings. The ethnic pantheon carries the world-view, philosophy, and religion of the people. In Soyinka, Ogun becomes the poet's persona as I have tried to do with Ivwri, the warrior god of the Urhobo people.

v) **Closeness to and importance of land reflect the African's sense of belonging and identity.** In Kenya's recent past, if you had a Mercedes Benz car but no piece of land to call yours, you were still considered to be poor.
vi) **African folklore** – folk tales, myths, legends, proverbs and songs infuse modern African literature with motifs, themes, characters, and techniques. No writer in modern times has used as many proverbs as Achebe has done in both his *Things Fall Apart* and *Arrow of God*.
vii) **Ideas of time and space and how they affect literature** – repetition, reincarnation, and cyclical movement of plot in novels and poetry. Westerners see space differently, and their concept of time is generally linear.
viii) **The language of African literature** – Africans may be writing, for instance, in English, but their writing has its unique subtext, invariably informed by indigenous languages. This paradigm is bound to make American students aware of many "Englishes," so to speak, and help them to know that others use English effectively in their own way.

Putting racial origins aside, in many ways African-American literature compares well with African literature. It reflects as African literature and other Third World literatures also do the condition of a minority and marginalized people. The separate and related historical experiences of Africans and African-Americans tend to show in the literature. Both literatures reflect history; they are political, and they express black/white conflicts. Also, they deal with issues of poverty, self-assertion, and identity. As Africans try to assert themselves culturally following European colonization with its assimilative policies, so do African-Americans in their own way. Many blacks struggle against being absorbed into the American mainstream. The emancipation of blacks can be compared to the political independence of African states. From this perspective, the Harlem Renaissance and the Black Arts Movement can be compared to the Negritude movement in Africa. Issues of solidarity, kinship, and moral uprightness against an oppressing group are similar and have elicited similar responses. The Black Variety of English, as reflected especially in African-American poetry, is comparable to the African use of English in which the writer's indigenous language has a great effect. A good example is

Sonia Sanchez's *We A BaddDDD People*, in which ethnic dialect is strong.

I have had the opportunity to teach World Literature in American colleges. Appalling to me was the fact that the syllabi handed to me were totally based on Western literature, from ancient times to the present (1991). Understandably, I asked myself: where is the "world" in this literature? Until a few decades ago, there used to be a narrow concept of literature, one that saw only Western creations as making it to the "world" standard. Of course, I added works from Africa, Asia, the Caribbean, and South America. Paradoxically and to my utter satisfaction, the African text, *Things Fall Apart*, was most warmly received. I was not surprised that *The Norton Anthology of World Literature* that came out two years later had both Achebe's *Things Fall Apart* and Wole Soyinka's *Death and the King's Horseman*. Thus, to give a comprehensive view of "world literature" and to reflect the world in its totality, African literature deserves a place in the American school curriculum. *Things Fall Apart*, for example, provides the reader with a different perspective of Conrad's *Heart of Darkness*. As you may know, the books have stirred a debate that has exposed and sharpened the difference between Eurocentric and Afrocentric concepts and views of history.

Modern African literature has gained recognition worldwide through such classics as Achebe's *Things Fall Apart*, Ngugi's *Weep Not, Child*, Alan Paton's *Cry, the Beloved Country*, and Wole Soyinka's *Death and the King's Horseman*. Literary prizes won by African writers have reinforced this recognition. Wole Soyinka, Nadine Godimer, and Mafouz have won the Nobel Prize for literature. Ben Okri won the Booker Prize in London. Nurrudin Farah won the Neustadt Prize. Chinua Achebe and Niyi Osundare have been awarded the Commonwealth Poetry Prize. Though this recognition is relatively recent, it confirms a trend, started in the early 1980s, of lively literature moving from the metropolitan centres of London, Madrid, Paris, and Lisbon to the former colonies in Africa, the Caribbean, and South America. Even in a country like the United States, the rise of African-American voices from the early 1970s can be attributed to the infusion of the "other" into the literature.

It is generally recognized in scholarly circles that African literature is one of the most vibrant literatures in the world today. African writers have shown, in their writings, elegance of style, profundity of vision and mastery of craft. They thus deserve to be read on their own merit.

There should be discrimination on what should be selected from African literature for inclusion in the American school curriculum. Teachers should avoid texts like Amos Tutuola's which are seen as curios that should be included, but use progressive and revolutionary texts. Such works that subvert Western epistemology and promote the humanity of Africans should be recommended.

Expanding the curriculum of American schools to include disciplines of other cultures is a welcome development. Understanding another culture through its literature helps to make one become adequately informed. This will correspondingly make one more sensitive, accommodating, human, and humane. Exposure to African literature will help to break stereotypes about Africans in America. Including African literature will show that there is not only William Shakespeare, but also our "WS," Wole Soyinka, and others. Africans are also making contribution to the world of culture. This will help the self-esteem of African-Americans in their pride in the African heritage. Africans will be speaking for themselves about themselves and should be listened to. They are a people grappling with complex existential problems.

From peripheral to central considerations and based on my experience over the years, African literature will fly well with American students. My experience of teaching *Things Fall Apart*, *Death and the King's Horseman*, and African poetry, among others, has been very positive. It enriches them not only with necessary human values but gives them a deeper concept of literature as a discipline. The sooner this process of literature inclusion begins, the richer the human experience will become and the better world we will create for our children and the generations to come.

References and works cited

Achebe, Chinua. *Things Fall Apart*. London: Heinemann, 1958.
---. *Arrow of God*. London: Heinemann, 1964.
---. *Anthills of the Savannah*. Oxford: Heinemann, 1987.
Finnegan, Ruth. *Oral Literature in Africa*. Nairobi: OUP, 1976.
Irele, Abiola. *The African Experience in Literature and Ideology*. London: Heinemann, 1981.
Kunene, Mazisi. *The Ancestors and the Sacred Mountain*. London: Heinemann, 1982.

Mbiti, John S. *African Religions and Philosophy*. London: Heinemann, 1969.
Ngugi, wa Thiong'o. *Weep Not, Child*. London: Heinemann, 1964.
Ojaide, Tanure. *Poetic Imagination in Black Africa: Essays on African Poetry*. Durham, NC: Carolina Academic Press, 1996.
Soyinka, Wole. *The Interpreters*. London: Heinemann, 1970.
---. *Myth, Literature and the African World*. London: Cambridge UP, 1976.

X

How the Urhobo people see the world through art*

In the African world, the art of a people and their life symbiotically reflect each other. This is very true of Urhobo people whose art expresses the totality of life as they live and understand it. What Emmanuel Jegede says of the Yoruba is also true of the Urhobo whose art reflects the entire cycle of life – birth, initiation, marriage, procurement of chieftaincy titles, and death, among others. The art of the Urhobo people communicates their beliefs, world-view, and understanding of human existence. Their art is a metaphor for life. Questions of why we are here on earth can be gleaned from the people's art. In other words, Urhobo art reflects all aspects of Urhobo existence and the essence of life. For this symbiotic relationship between the people's art and their life, one can envision how the Urhobo people see the world through art.

The Urhobo, numbering about three million people, occupy mainly the western and northern fringes of the Niger River delta region of the present Delta State of Nigeria. Large pockets of Urhobo people also live in the contiguous states of Bayelsa, Rivers, and Edo and as immigrants in many Yoruba-speaking areas such as Ife, Lagos, and Okitipupa. Large communities of Urhobo migrants are now settled all over Nigeria, including Jos, Kano, Maiduguri, and Yola. Many have also settled in Cote d'Ivoire, Ghana, and Liberia. There is a considerable Urhobo immigrant population in England and the United States.

The Urhobo in their present environment are said to be an amalgam of different waves of migrating groups and an indigenous group that

---

* Presented at the National African Museum of the Smithsonian Institution in Washington, DC, on Saturday, November 18, 2000. Also reprinted in *Where Gods and Mortals Meet: The Art of the Urhobo People* edited by Perkins Foss.

absorbed them. The main group migrated from the Edo region, where they had settled in a space called "Aka" (associated with Benin) and had been forced to migrate at different periods during the tyrannical Ogiso dynasty. Oral history and myths are still replete with stories of Urhobo people being selectively used for human sacrifice by the Obas, and this led to their escape by land and rivers through areas like Abraka, Ologbo, and along the Niger River. At least one group migrated from the Ijo area through the Amasuoma clan. There also appears, from Urhobo vocabulary, some remote Igbo connection, which could be because of the period of migration along the Niger River and proximity to the western Igbo group of Ukwuani. Onigu Otite's The Urhobo People has a detailed historiography of Urhobo, taking into account Hubbard's colonial work, Egharevba's study of Benin and neighbouring groups, and Obaro Ikime's study of the Niger-Delta peoples.

The Urhobo now occupy some twenty-two clans/kingdoms that can easily be divided into southern and northern terrains. The southern Urhobo people border on the Ijo, Isoko, and Itsekiri. These live across mangrove swamps and very luxuriant rain forests. The major occupations of these groups of Urhobo are fishing, hunting, and farming. Those to their north, far from the wide rivers but still riverine, also farm, hunt, and fish. Nowadays, many Urhobo live in urban areas such as Sapele and Ughelli, and form the overwhelming majority in the politically contested town of Warri. The urban Urhobo are mainly traders.

For the purpose of this study, it is important to summarize some traits of the Urhobo people. According to Otite and from personal observation, the people are very republican in character, a euphemism for their individualism that even today makes them to "rebel against autocracy" (Otite 20). The frequent common Urhobo utterance, "We gher' ovwe?" ("Do you feed me?"), clearly registers each person's belief in self-reliance. This is inextricably tied to their concept of honour and pride. They are a highly industrious people, a virtue, which has led to the success of many as migrants inside and outside Nigeria.

While there is a sense of ethnic belonging, the Urhobo people are not as cohesive as many other Nigerian ethnic groups. One reason could be the disparate groups that Mukoro Mowoe glued together into one ethnic association. The Isoko people have broken away to ascertain their own ethnic autonomy. The Okpe, a large fragment of the ethnic group, are unsure of whether they are real Urhobo or a different group

– at different times in the past they asserted their difference by saying they were not Urhobo. The presence of many and at times not mutually comprehensible dialects of the language, lack of a common festival, and absence of a single traditional ruler have all helped to fragment the psyche of the Urhobo people. To most other Urhobo people, especially those in Agbarho, Agbon and Ughelli areas, Effurun and Okpe dialects are incomprehensible. Ironically, it is easier for these groups to understand Isoko than some dialects of their own Urhobo language. The people therefore do not have the cohesive spirit of, for instance, the Bini or the Itsekiri.

However, despite this republican spirit of the people, they are very communal in many ways. There are still common ponds and farming areas, among other forms of communal cooperation. The common festivals of some clans/kingdoms also cater for the spiritual interest of the people. The extended family practice still continues.

To the Urhobo, there are two worlds: the physical, natural world and the metaphysical invisible world of ancestors, spirits, gods, and witches. In Urhobo thought, this physical world and the other (spiritual) world contrast and parallel each other. As John Mbiti says of African peoples, the Urhobo are a very spiritual people. Many believe that ailments are due to natural transgressions. Thus, when somebody is sick, they traditionally seek a diviner to tell what has led to the condition. Usually, sacrifices and herbal prescriptions are recommended. To the traditional Urhobo, there is rarely a natural death – a spiritual explanation is always given to a death or misfortune. People, therefore, try their best to live spiritually clean lives since spiritual transgressions have their karmic repercussions. A woman who flirted would confess her "stepping outside" of her matrimonial home or, according to popular belief, she could die from child delivery. Sometimes, in Urhobo belief, the sins of the mother are visited on her children who can become sick or even die. Witches who do evil somehow suffer the repercussion of their acts. People therefore join religious sects, like *igbe*, or do protective medicines to cater for their physical and spiritual salvation. Clans have festivals to exorcise evil spirits for communal health and prosperity.

There is no single Urhobo religion, but many forms of traditional religion exist especially in the form of ancestor-worship and religious sects like *igbe* and varieties of shrine worship (*orha*). The people believe in a Supreme God, who can be approached directly and through smaller gods and ancestors for their well-being. In Urhobo traditional belief, people before they are born make their choices of what they will be in life at Urhoro and basically live accordingly. The ideal life should involve good health, many children, prosperity/wealth, and long life. These are the "gifts" prayed for with cola nuts on religious and social occasions. There is belief in reincarnation, that people are born, they die, and are born again in an unending cycle of life. Underlying these beliefs is the need to do good things, since evil will not escape punishment. Also as those who are good in this life will be rewarded in the next life, so will those who do evil suffer punishment in the afterlife.

These spiritual beliefs also underlie the so much attention paid to burial ceremonies in Urhoboland. In addition to the pride and honour of the family, it is generally believed that a good burial would help the deceased to make a better choice in his or her return to this life.

In order to understand how the Urhobo people see the world through art, certain basic concepts need to be defined. Four interconnected terms easily come to mind: *akpo* and *erivwin*, and *edjo* and *oma*. The word *akpo* is very loaded in Urhobo philosophy. It means "life," a spiritual phenomenon. The Urhobo go as far as to say *owho r'akpo* to designate the "living." Thus *akpo* is the counterpoint of *erivwin* and *ughwu*, death; hence *owho erivwin* (dead person, ghost, or spirit). This shows the close connection of the physical and spiritual worlds, a duality that I will later expatiate upon.

Akpo also means "world," the human existence; the physical world we live in. This definition also embraces, for the Urhobo, culture, society, lifestyle, and other socio-cultural aspects of the people's lives. The old people talk of *akpo aware* and *akpo oke na*; the old and the modern times respectively. There is the general association of the old with the authentic and the modern/new with corrupting changes from outside, first colonization and then contemporary influences.

Thus, the title of this chapter might as well read "How the Urhobo see life through art," since *akpo* means "world," "life," and "customs." Life in this world means human existence. One lives in a particular space and a particular time to have human experience. By akpo the Urhobo express the physical and spiritual nature of life as well as the entire socio-cultural aspects of their lives.

In order for the patriarchal Urhobo to live a normal life, which entails having good health and long life, children, and prosperity, he attempts to ward off evil forces that originate from witches and evil spirits. He knows that he has made his choices at *Urhoro*, but most people seem to believe that their choices were positive and only envious and evil persons and spirits want them not to realize those goals. To counteract evil and agents of *erivwin*, they attempt to fortify themselves against negative forces, which they believe co-exist with positive forces. In this effort, they have *ebo* ("medicines") and *edjo* (shrines) to protect them.

Usually, the medicines and shrines involve *oma/ekaro*, artistic creations that are invested with spiritual power – these are usually sculptures. *Oma* traditionally means something molded out of clay; some are fired and others not. *Ekaro* uses wood as material. However, *oma* seems to be currently used all over Urhobo to designate sculpture, carved or moulded. In any case, the physical represents the spiritual; the human-made represents divine manifestation.

To the traditional Urhobo people, therefore, art and ritual go together. Sacrifices and festivals all over Urhobo are meant to exorcise evil spirits from communities. These are expected to bring about renewal and rebirth of communal spirit. The festivals take place once a year and often during the raining season – a symbolic cleansing. By this the Urhobo re-validate the values that give meaning to them as a group and assist them to maintain coherence of the group. There is a delicate balance, which allows the individual to remain free from and yet bound to the community to be able to be in good standing in both the physical and the spiritual worlds.

The duality of things is also affirmed in art related to ritual. *Edjo* and *oma/ekaro* are sometimes used interchangeably. However, *oma* is wood that when sculpted becomes the home of *edjo*, god or spirit. In any case, *oma* and *edjo* are wood and spirit, a duality that is comparable to life/birth and death, humans and spirits. In Urhobo cosmology, there is a correspondence of different forces. Nature in the form of wood is infused with life and spirit in a consecrating ritual. Among Urhobo medicine men and sculptors, certain rituals are performed before either a tree is cut down or its bark is removed. The case of the mythical *akpobrisi* tree comes to mind – this is a tree that is covered with climbers and said to allow no other trees around, and is the symbol of tyranny in nature. Anybody trying to cut the bark of an *akpobrisi* tree strips before its presence and races away as soon as he cuts off the part of the tree he wants. According to traditional belief, the evil spirit in the tree pursues such a person but cannot recognize him once he has put back his clothes.

The Urhobo traditionally do not see what others, especially in the West, call their "art" as something beautiful, even though they have certain aesthetic criteria in mind. The people recognize excellence in artistry in *owena*, a great craftsman. The so-called art or sculpture has its function and value in the performance of ritual for the well-being of the individual or the community. In fact, when it comes to sculptures and other artistic creations related to rituals, art is in Urhobo seen as ugly. People are compared to *oma* and *edjo* to denote their physical ugliness or sour looks.

In the *Udje* dance song tradition, *oma* is often alluded to, to describe persons. In "Aruviere," "*akare oshare/osho gbagbaragba*" (they carved a man/with an erect penis) to induce suitors to an ugly and unappealing young lady. Significantly, the male statuette assumed life and humanity and demanded Aruviere for "himself." The spirit invoked into the wood has taken a life of its own. Another song describes Rherheyere as "*edjo r'Urhobo rhie Evwere re*." Here *edjo* means "*umiovwo*", ugliness. The Ijo people warned Rherheyere that should he visit their town again, they would sacrifice him to their god because of his ugly looks. Different *erha/edjo/ema* (shrines and sculptures) as *Ogbaurhie* of Otujevwe, *Igbewha* of Otokutu, and *Echeha* of Ekakpamre are used as symbols of ugliness.

There is a certain ambiguity of the Urhobo when it comes to *edjo*, which they invest with divinity and want to save them but at the same time consider ugly. While aware of the spirit behind the matter, Memerume of Edjophe says "*Oma j'ekpe*"; that is, a mould is mere clay. This shows that even the divine is fallible among humans, because the mould can dissolve, as the wood will disintegrate with time. Ironically, humans survive the *oma* and the *edjo* to recreate new symbols of divine manifestation. Power and weakness are enshrined in the people's god. An Urhobo saying is: "*Esia amwa n'edjo, edjo k'ubrurhe*" (If you remove the cloth from the *edjo*, it becomes a mere piece of wood).

The Urhobo dress their *edjo* (spirits) with either *ukpebo* (white) or *ibosu/ododo* (red). Usually, white represents those gods or spirits like *edjo-ame* that are for peace, fertility, and good health. Red on the shrine designates more aggressive gods or spirits like Ivwri, Egba, or other warrior gods. Usually, priests or servers of the shrine splash blood of the sacrificed animal on the cloth used to cover the shrine. There is an Urhobo saying that the cloth used in dressing a god is never washed before it tears off. Warrior shrines like Egba, Ivwri, and Ovu-ughere show the Urhobo as a people who see the world and life as fraught with hostile forces and perils; hence they seek spiritual and supernatural powers to overcome them for a peaceful life.

Significantly, art becomes a metaphor in Urhobo for the relationship between the inside and the outside. The sculpture of a god or ancestor may be made of wood or clay, but it has potency in the spirit that resides therein. In other words, the inside is what matters and not so much the outside of things. This sums up the general Urhobo preference for the internal beauty of character, rather than the outside superficial beauty of the skin.

The Urhobo people use art as a metaphor for their existential struggles. The various *ema* and *edjo* in multiple ways elicit the fears and hopes of the people. From their art, the following can be said of how the Urhobo see the world and life:

- The Urhobo people see themselves as living in two worlds – the physical and metaphysical. The two worlds contrast and parallel each other.
- Urhobo art is a moral medium, as the various shrines and other icons of worship espouse good deeds, since evil has its respective consequences. The Urhobo see the world as sanctioning a moral imperative for humans. Those who do good will be rewarded and those who do evil will be punished either in this world or in the next world. This makes people humble and encourages them to do good almost all the time.
- They see the world in terms of dualities – physical and spiritual, good and bad, life and death. Binary divisions are there but not rigid. In folk tales, humans and spirits meet and enter the other's world with different consequences.
- The Urhobo see the ideal of human existence as a communal one because of the solidarity, support, and social cohesion involved. To them, there is strength in numbers; hence people boast about the sizes of their families. Families and communities have shrines in which they perform sacrifices for their well-being.
- The individual is separate and yet bonded to a community. Individuals have their own medicines and shrines for individual interests, as there are family or community *edjo* to bring cohesiveness and sense of solidarity to the group.
- The Urhobo see the world as full of dangers that have to be combated with supernatural forces for a happy life. The examples

of the communal Egba, Ivwri, and Ovu-ughere, among others, show this coming together as a group to be strong and be better able to fight off aggression.
- The Urhobo maintain a certain ambiguity toward the divine and supernatural in their arts. The *edjo* is at once a saviour and at the same time a symbol of ugliness. The devotees may not like it physically but it is a necessary potent force to counter physical and spiritual forms of aggression. The divine in being invested in wood or clay that disintegrates with time and very fast in the humid Urhobo climate is made fallible. Humans invest divinity when the wood is consecrated and the divinity could be removed. Humans commission new gods when they so desire.
- The art of the people communicates their ideals of human existence – good health and long life, many children that will perpetuate the family name, and prosperity. The art also communicates the Urhobo love of beauty/handsomeness, dignity, wealth, and high status, among others.
- Though a patriarchy in which men seem to enjoy more privileges than women, the art shows how the people see the importance of women. In masquerade performances, the *oni-edjo* comes in to perform after the *emo-edjo* warmed the arena. In art there is promotion of the balance between male and female, parent and child to emphasize humanity.
- Ritual and art go together in the lives of the people.
- Reciprocity ensures cordial relationship between the ancestors/gods and humans and also among human beings. The ancestors and gods guide and guard the living who correspondingly offer them service and sacrifices, especially at festival times – mashed yam (*emare*), bones, and blood of sacrificed animals. To the Urhobo people, "*erue emu k'owho k'arie*" (one should be appreciative of kindness).
- There is a time for everything. The saying, "*ukpe te, ke rue emu r'ukpe*" (when the time comes, you do what is due). In other words, there is an order pervading the universe that should not be broken. The *edjo* come out at their time; sacrifices are performed before the *erha* (shrines) at the appropriate season.
- The Urhobo people through art see the world in hierarchical terms as shown in artistic vocabulary of, for example, *oni-edjo* (the mother-mask), *ose-emo* (father-of-children mask), and *ini-ide*

(grandmother masks) in festival times. The *oni-edjo* comes last in masquerade performances.
- The world is seen as intricately connected by parallel, reciprocating, and mutually co-existing forces. The gods, spirits, and ancestors need the living as the living need them. This is a metaphor for life – no single person is self-sufficient but is complemented by others. Urhobo art affirms faith in the communal and cohesive lives of its people struggling with existential problems with help from fellow human beings and the supernatural. Collaboration is a pre-requisite of life.
- Urhobo art reflects the people's concept of life in its totality.

References

Alagoa, Ebiegberi. *A History of the Niger Delta.* Ibadan: Ibadan UP, 1972.
Clark-Bekederemo, J.P., ed. *The Ozidi Saga: Collected and Translated from the Oral Ijo Version of Okabou Ojobolo.* Washington, DC: Howard UP, 1991.
D'Azevedo, Warren., ed. *The Traditional Artist in African Societies.* Bloomington: Indiana UP, 1989.
Ikime, Obaro, *Niger Delta Rivalry: Itsekiri-Urhobo Relations and the European Presence, 1884-1936.* London: Longman, 1969.
Mbiti, John S. *African Religions and Philosophy.* London: Heinemann, 1969.
Ojaide, Tanure with S.S. Ugheteni. *Yono Urhobo.* Lagos: Macmillan, 1983.
--- *Poetic Imagination in Black Africa.* Durham, NC: Carolina Academic Press, 1996.
Okpewho, Isidore, *The Epic in Africa.* NY: Columbia UP, 1989.
---. *African Oral Literature: Background, Character, and Continuity.* Bloomington: Indiana UP, 1992.
Ong, Walter J., *Orality and Literacy: The Technologizing of the Word.* London/New York: Methuen, 1982.
Osaghae, Eghosa, "Ethnic Minorities and Federalism in Nigeria," *African Affairs* 90 (1991): 237- 58.
Otite, Onigu (ed.), *The Urhobo People,* Ibadan: Heinemann, 1983.
Thompson, Stith. *Motif-Index of Folk-Literature.* Bloomington: Indiana UP, 1989.

XI

Countering terror in the literary world: the experience of activism*

Terror in one form or another is pervasive worldwide. It is a societal phenomenon, a demon that writers experience and confront in their daily lives. After all, literature is, according to Robert Hodge, a "mode of discourse that shares...a common ground in social experience and cultural practice" (quoted in Irele xiv). Life inspires art and art reflects life. Writers are not air plants, but humans rooted in place and time. They are part of and share in society's problems and challenges. Terror manifests itself in many forms; some more visible and dramatic than others. The most obvious and visible are violence, war, and loud expressions of hate. Terror can also manifest itself in the forms of repression, persecution, denial of fundamental human rights, or any acts meant to instil fear and/or anxiety on one or more people to cower them into subservience or submission. The means of unleashing terror include surveillance, harassment, arrest, imprisonment, beating, and killing or execution. In the literary world, it can also involve censorship and banning from publishing or airing those individual views that are different from official or state-sanctioned ones.

In most cases, terror is inflicted by one who assumes (or presumes) that the "other" (the victim) is not living by certain "standards," usually prejudiced or extreme, and so attempts to coerce the "deviant" other into his or her way. Sometimes terror is unleashed against a person or people who are hated. Many use terror as a weapon to bargain for rights, power, status, or other political, social and economic advantages. The Irish Republican Army, ETA of Spain, Palestinian

---

* Being the James W. Moore Lecture delivered at Millikin University, Decatur, IL 62522 on November 28, 2001.

groups, and the Egbesu Boys of the Niger Delta of Nigeria, among others, wield terror in their struggle for a cause. I will like to emphasize that the Niger Delta group was formed in response to state-sponsored exploitation and terrorism; hence it was "reactive." The military government refused to negotiate with the group and the Egbesu Boys had to wield terror in their struggle for a cause.

The terrorizer or terrorist often resorts to images and other modes of discourse and representation that demonize or devalue the other to establish the cultural and moral authority to perpetrate terror. This is both ironical and paradoxical because of the evil intent and act involved. There are, thus, moral and ethical dimensions to terrorism, as it pertains to issues of right or wrong. However, it is questionable whether any form of terror or violence can be morally acceptable even if it is for a just cause. Can one argue that it is ethical for one to use means of terror to achieve a goal? It is my personal view though that when one is tired of turning the other cheek as a victim of terror, one can take any means necessary, including violence, to end the pain. Let me acknowledge that in many situations "terror" is a relative tag. It is often said that one person's terrorist is another person's freedom fighter. One does not need to go to the murky situation in the Middle East for examples. Some of the militia groups in the United States – and their sympathizers – saw the FBI raid on the Branch Davidians in Waco, Texas, as terrorism. Also many activist African Americans saw the MOVE raid in Philadelphia in the same light. Terrorism is arguably, therefore, sometimes a case of positionality.

Whatever the source or means, terror is mainly physical and psychological. People are killed, executed, maimed, or disabled. Victims and survivors live with the trauma of terror by not leading normal lives and often develop nightmares or other forms of emotional dysfunction.

It is in society in which terror is a daily reality that the writer lives and draws inspiration for poems, fiction, and plays. Of course, the inspiration comes from experiences around or imagined, and terror is often there for those bothered by it to write on or be conditioned by. Writers over the ages have encountered in a personal or collective way the experience of terror and have through writing and activism attempted to eliminate it in their time, prevent a future recurrence, or assist its victims spiritually.

Writers use courage, persistence, sacrifice, and martyrdom to confront perpetrators of evil and terror to embarrass them so as to desist from further evil. Literature delineates the conflict between good and evil, and puts evil/terror on the defensive. By taking on individuals, groups, and governments that use machines of terror, writers risk imprisonment, exile, and execution. However, being on the side of life, activist writers make their readers more sensitive to suffering and issues of injustice that need to be tackled. Sensitized, the society becomes more humane. Writers have, thus, consistently posed imaginative and ideological challenges to terror and its apparatus in their promotion and affirmation of human and spiritual values. While this exposes the problematic relation between art and ideology, form and content, and the aesthetic and the ethical in art, countering terror confirms the moral significance of the writer.

In their vision many writers have prophesied terror in the form of war, as done by the Nigerian Christopher Okigbo in *Path of Thunder*. W.B. Yeats in "The Second Coming" foresees a "beast" slouching toward humankind, an apocalyptic calamity that presaged World Wars I and II. Rainer Maria Rilke in his *Duino Elegies* sees fascism as terror. So writers have always used the metaphors of beast and terror to symbiotically refer to the same thing. Thus, many writers have taken it as part of their mission to counter terror that involves persons, societies, or humankind. Some do it only in their writings in direct didactic ways or in very subtle style; others do it both in and out of their writings and make their activism and practical ideology reinforce their writing.

At this juncture, let me summarize what the literary art means to different writers and their audience based on cultural attitudes. The West has generally in modern times advocated a tradition of art for art's sake based on the people's sense of individual responsibility. On the other hand, in traditional and modern Africa, the literary tradition (like other arts) is functional and based on the premise of a collective destiny of the people. While proponents of art for art's sake put premium on form over content, exponents of utilitarian art place more significance on content than on form. We are, therefore, more likely to see those who see art as functional combining discourse and praxis to place their writings at the service of a cause. Carl von Clausewitz sees the latter type of literature as "politics by other means" (qtd. in Irele 52). There is a lot of rhetoric, militancy, and ideological activity in those who use literature for a cause, which they also espouse outside.

George Orwell says that every writer attempts to move the world in a certain direction and his *1984* arose from his fears of totalitarianism, a form of terror. However, the activist/ideological stance is not so much in the American tradition; it is there only at the margin. This is perhaps because of the relative stability in political and economic spheres. While this may be true of white male middle-class writers, there are ideologically committed American writers, especially among African-American ones. I will expatiate on this later. Outside of America, even in Europe and especially in the Third World, this ideology-driven art is rampant because of tyranny through dictatorship.

I will proceed to discuss areas in which terror has been perpetrated and how literature has presented it and at the same time countered it.

The political system is a major area of terror inflicted on the writer, society, and humankind. There is a long history of this, ranging from lack of democracy to military dictatorship. A few examples will illustrate terror as a weapon of both terrorizing party and victim. In the Stalinist era, Stalin unleashed terror against non-conformist writers and citizens. Osip Mandelstam, in particular, suffered for writing against tyranny and in a subtle way referring to Stalin as the "Kremlin mountaineer." He was sent to a labor camp, where his health failed and he died. In the Stalinist era and subsequent Soviet regimes, non-conformist writers were banned from being published, and their works not sold in the country. Boris Pasternak's *Doctor Zgivago* was one of such as many of Alexander Solhzenitsyn's books for a long time. Most so-called dissident writers were sent into exile or thrown into the "gulag."

Though this sort of political atmosphere breeds self-censorship, as the writers want to prevent themselves from persecution and libel, they still write. In the Soviet example, the writers thought of obscure metaphors and symbols to describe the personalities responsible for the terror.

The apartheid system in South Africa for decades before the election of Nelson Mandela was built on terror. African, "colored," and a few white writers (such as Nadine Godimer) during the apartheid period used their talent to lash at the terror of apartheid. Perhaps the most articulate of them was Dennis Brutus, who waged a relentless three-pronged war against the system: embarrass its perpetrators, expose its evil to the outside world, and fill its African victims with hope of freedom. He exposes the brutality and sadism of apartheid as in "The sounds begin again":

the siren in the night
the thunder at the door

the shriek of nerves in pain.

Then the keening crescendo
of faces split by pain
the wordless, endless wail
only the unfree know. (19)

With Brutus, life and art conjoin in the poetry. In one poem, he writes:

More terrible than any beast
that can be tamed or bribed
the iron monster of the world
ingests me in its grinding maw (7).

Of course, apartheid was the "iron monster," the terror machine. Brutus condemns the "impregnation of our air / with militarism" (78). As head of the South African Non-Racial Olympic Committee (SANROC), he kept South Africa and then Rhodesia out of international sports. He relishes his success in "Let me say it": "I have lashed them / the marks of my scars / lie deep in their psyche" (89) and he calls the perpetrators of apartheid "these thieves." With such name-calling and strong images, the poet made perpetrators of apartheid feel guilty. Dennis Brutus is a sterling example of the activist poet who has successfully countered a system of terror.

Military or civilian dictatorship is a phenomenon that has gripped many African and Third World countries from the late 1960s to the present. Nigeria's Wole Soyinka has struggled against military dictatorship from the 1960s to recent times. During the Nigerian civil war of 1967-1970, he was jailed for condemning the killing of Igbo people and attempting to avert more killings. His *Shuttle in the Crypt*, *The Man Died*, and *Ogun Abibiman* are art placed at the service of activism against forms of terror in Nigeria and South Africa respectively. Soyinka was a member of the National Democratic Coalition (NADECO) whose aim was to fight the excesses and atrocities of Sani Abacha – judicial murders, assassinations, jailing, torture, and executions perpetrated to silence Nigerians into acceptance of a diabolic despotism. There are other examples from Nigeria and other African countries. Much of contemporary African literature deals with the criticism of corrupt and despotic regimes on the continent.

The political economic system based on exploitation, repression, and oppression instils terror on subjects/citizens. In many corrupt countries, a clique manipulates the economy to its advantage to the total neglect and detriment of the common people. In such a society, the gap between the few haves and the majority have-nots is very wide. The authorities use repressive measures and intimidation to maintain the status quo, which favours them. This is a form of terror as in Kenya, which many writers such as Ngugi wa Thiong'o and Jared Angira with ideological inclinations have stood up to challenge.

Let me take the case of Ngugi versus the Kenyan Government. As a result of the prevailing politico-economic situation in his country and moved by what he considered to be the state's terrorism, Ngugi started to espouse Marxist ideas as an alternative system. Ngugi has used his literary art to range on the side of the oppressed peasants, workers, and students. Starting from colonial times when Britain seized lands from native Kenyans and distributed them among its white settlers, the economic discrepancies have survived through independent Kenya. In his activist role, Ngugi accepted an invitation from the women of the Kamiriithu Community Education and Cultural Centre to establish a native language theatre, which resulted in the writing and production of *I Will Marry When I Want* in Gikuyu language. The theatre was so successful in reaching the common people that the government panicked that the author was stirring discontent against it. Ngugi was arrested in December 1977 and jailed in 1978 and went into exile after being released some three years later. Ngugi turned from writing in English to writing in his indigenous Gikuyu and Swahili to reach more people. He used this not only to sharpen the consciousness of his people but also to counter what he considered to be Kenyan cultural genocide in the use of English by only the Kenyan elite class. Ngugi's response to politico-economic state terror against his people was to counter it with Marxist ideology and cultural nationalist ideals. Arrest and detention are conventional tools of terror to prevent the writer from self-expression. Ngugi succeeded in drawing world attention to the one-party despotism in Kenya, and years later international financial organizations tied assistance to Kenya with improvement in political pluralism.

Religious fanaticism breeds terror and terrorism. Recent happenings since September 11, 2001 have forced into the open a phenomenon that has become troubling over the years. Salman Rushdie, Wole Soyinka, and V.S. Naipaul have, in their respective ways at different times in the past, warned against the dangers of Islamic, Christian, and other kinds of religious extremism. The plight of Rushdie with a *fatwa*, death sentence, placed on him by the late Ayatollah Khomeini, has exemplified in practical terms the stark reality of terror.

Let me present the case of Egypt's Naguib Mahfouz whose Nobel Prize is no amulet against the relentless attacks of militant Islamist groups. They have successfully ensured the banning order on *Gablawi's Children*, first issued in 1959, is retained. According to *Index on Censorship*, "Their own publications include virulent attacks on Mahfouz insisting that he will burn in Hell for the book. Their cartoons constantly depict the author walking into the fires of Hell with copies of his novels" (*Index*, May/June 1994, 118). When in 1989 renewed attempts were made to un-ban *Gablawi's Children* and the monthly *Al Yasar* started to serialize it, the "Islamist press campaigned so virulently to have the serialization stopped that Mahfouz himself asked the magazine to stop the serialization. By this stage Sheikh Omar Abdul Rahman, the spiritual leader of *Gamaat Islamia*, had issued a *fatwa* excommunicating the author and calling on him to repent having written the novel and to denounce it" (118). What could be a worse act of terror or terrorism than this? Once Omar's mullahs succeeded with Mahfouz, they became even bolder in challenging the imagination of writers.

Also in Egypt, Nawal El Saadawi, in 2001, had her marriage of over two decades annulled by an Islamic court because her husband was not a Muslim – pay-back for her outspoken remarks and writings against the treatment of women in some Islamic societies. Of recent, a young and bright Egyptian poet, Iman Mirsal, left for Canada, perhaps to be free of fundamentalist terror. Critics and fundamentalists have remarked that she was writing poetry unprecedented of an Islamic woman – blatantly acknowledging pre-marital sex, flirtation, and describing the woman's body. A Bangla Deshi female writer literally fled her country to Sweden for refuge when Islamic fundamentalists threatened her life because of her writings.

Issues of persecution, oppression, and denial of rights of women are closely linked to religious and/or social orthodoxy, the latter sometimes coalescing with the former in traditional patriarchies. In other words, women currently live under terror more in many Islamic and patriarchal societies than elsewhere. This also explains the condition of many African women who might have experienced female circumcision, a form of terror, writing against it. The Nigerian playwright Juliana Okoh has in several plays dealt with the trauma and emotional disabling effect on circumcised women. In recent years, the State Assemblies of Bayelsa and Delta in Nigeria have banned female circumcision.

Minority groups among a largely majority ethnic nation tend to suffer from abuse in the sphere of cultural rights and are terrorized consistently in their attempts to express themselves. As in Turkey and Algeria, the central governments with legislative power and state authority ban minority languages from being used in their effort to present a cohesive rather than a multi-ethnic and diverse image of the nation. This is the case of the Kurds in Turkey and the Berbers in Algeria. Their leaders have been jailed and the Kurds have a resistant movement, whose leader, Abdullah Ocalan, was captured a few years ago and has been condemned to death. Berber resistance has been in the form of demonstrations in their cities for the recognition of their language. In both cases, the state has recently made a few concessions on the ethnic languages.

This phenomenon of majority groups terrorizing minority groups is present in Kashmir/India and Nigeria's oil-rich Niger Delta. In addition to resisting Indian hegemony over Kashmir, Agha Shahid Ali, as in *The Country Without a Post Office*, is active in exposing the plight of his subjugated people. Similarly, Ken Saro-Wiwa brought attention of the world to Ogoniland and the minority groups of the Niger Delta, where Nigeria's oil wealth comes from. He set his stories and novels in Dukana, an Ogoni town, and collected Ogoni folktales in the effort to resist the silencing and erasure of his people from Nigeria's cultural life. In fact, through the activism of writers among others, UNESCO adopted a Universal Declaration on the World's Indigenous Peoples.

There is environmental terror in many parts of the world. Literary writers worldwide are some of the most conscious of environmental matters and so use their writings and activism to advance the case for a healthy environment. Nowhere is this environmental terror unleashed with impunity than the Niger Delta area of Nigeria.

Shell and other multinational oil companies such as Texaco, Chevron, Total, and Elf have prospected for oil in the area for over forty years. As a result of the oil exploration and gas flaring, the rivers are polluted and dead from oil slicks; the farm lands destroyed with frequent oil spills; villages burnt; and there have been outbreaks of mysterious and fatal diseases. Shell, in particular, has allied itself with successive military dictators in Nigeria to ignore the complaints of the local people, minority groups, while it increases its profit margins.

Shell asks the Nigerian government to send soldiers to guard their facilities and they end up shooting indiscriminately at peaceful demonstrators.

As a result of Saro-Wiwa's activism against this terror, he was framed and hanged on November 10, 1996. The ITV documentary, "The Drilling Field," testifies to the horrendous terror of the alliance of a multinational oil conglomerate and a dictatorial government against helpless groups of the Niger Delta. Through writings of Saro-Wiwa in particular, but also of Isidore Okpewho in *Tides* and the writer's *Labyrinths of the Delta* and *Delta Blues* the issue of the degradation of the Niger Delta environment is addressed. Through writing and activism there is now established by the Nigerian Government a Niger Delta Development Corporation to restore the environment, create jobs for the farmers, fishermen, and hunters whose means of sustenance have been devastated by the oil greed of Shell and the Nigerian government.

There is terror worldwide. While I have up till now named instances of terror outside the United States, there are local instances of terror. As stated earlier, every writer lives in a society with one form or the other of terror. Terror is unleashed against advocates of choice, and there have been violent actions taken against doctors who perform abortion, as also against the women who seek to exercise their rights. Racism and anti-Semitism are forms of terror against mainly blacks and Jews respectively. Sexism and homophobia are terrorizing attitudes. Stigmatizing because of a disability or a disease such as HIV/AIDS is an act of terror, as are spousal abuse and rape. American writers have dealt exhaustively with issues of racism and homophobia as African-American and gay and lesbian writers have carried their plight into the forefront of the literary debate and readership's presence.

However, there are writers like other artists, who advocate art for art's sake and feel that it is outside the realm of the artist to be political or activist. There has since the early 1970s been the profusion of confessional writings, especially in poetry and memoirs, which reflect this American trend. There are critics of the canon who talk of "extra-literary" materials and see African writers, to quote Chinua Achebe, as too earnest, too serious, and too activist. Of course, there are exceptions to this. Gary Snyder, for instance, has consistently championed the environment and spirituality. James Baldwin, Ishmael Reed, Amiri Baraka, Nikki Giovanni, Sonia Sanchez, and Toni Morrison, among others, are activists in various ways. Their respective works reflect predicators of socio-political commitment in American literature. Morrison, for example, has written on the damage done to the African-American psyche by racism as in *The Bluest Eye*.

The point needs to be made that those who are silent in the face of terror against fellow Americans or human beings are taking a political position – they are supporting terrorists. So, the silences of a writer could be very subliminal and reveal much about him or her. The situation in which writers close themselves to society and immerse in the self may be due to the Western tradition of individual responsibility that advocates art for art's sake and, in recent centuries, places form over content. In any case, in Western countries where there have been dictatorships as in Greece, Portugal, and Spain, writers have been activists in and out of their writings, as has been the case in East European countries under communism. Odysseus Elytis and Garcia Lorca are good examples.

Writers, through their writings, assume certain roles to contribute to the development of their individual societies. Usually the writer becomes the orphans' shield. Literature from the experience of Mandelstam, Rilke, Garcia Lorca, Vaclav Havel, Brutus, Soyinka, Saro-Wiwa, and El Saadawi, among so many others, functions as the voice of the voiceless and silenced to speak out against terror. Writers are at the vanguard in the struggle of the oppressed, exploited, persecuted, dispossessed, enslaved, and terrorized to gain freedom, justice, and peace. Many writers assume the role of "orphans' shield" in and out of writing. With these writers, nobody is really safe if one person or group is being terrorized.

Writers form the opposition against evil, tyranny, and all forms of terror. Literature affirms life and humanity in theory, practice, and the activist life of the writer. As the antithesis to terror, literature and its writers are invaluable to growth and sustenance of civilization not only in the cultural production but also in making human beings more sensitive and so considerate of others. As Gunter Grass reminds the world of the militant Islamists in Egypt as far back as 1994, "If the mullahs...succeed in gagging the storytellers so that we have a world without them, then the history of humanity has not been fully told, and is at an end" (*Index*, May/June 1994, back cover).

Activism on the part of writers has resulted in many successes against multiple forms of terror. Brutus in SANROC, Saro-Wiwa in MOSOP, and Soyinka in NADECO employ their "extra-literary" callings to reinforce the writing mission. The expulsion of apartheid

South Africa from international sports and the eventual collapse of apartheid, the fall of the Nigerian military dictatorship, and the establishment of the Niger Delta Development Corporation all attest to the effects of activism in countering terror, overthrowing evil, and in its place installing humane systems.

Related to activism and its mobilization strategy, literature makes the local global and simultaneously the global local. Exposure through books and the Internet, where poems, stories, memoirs, and novels are posted, sharpens the consciousness of people. In a period of globalization, the more people of diverse walks of life and nations learn about problems of one place, the more human values will be defended against perpetrators of terror. Writing has always had transnational effects on people by broadening and deepening their consciousness. During the ethnic cleansing in Bosnia-Hercegovina, Salman Rushdie saw himself as an "imaginary citizen" of Sarajevo to emphasize the need for empathy and solidarity with victims to combat terror.

For ages, writers have assumed the role of prophet in their individual societies. I have earlier mentioned W.B. Yeats who wrote about the beast of the Second Coming, which can be interpreted as not so much Christ but about World Wars I and II. In *Path of Thunder*, Nigeria's Okigbo prophesied war in: "Thunder can break – Earth, bind me fast – / Obduracy, the disease of elephants" (63) and

> And the secret thing in its heaving
> Threatens with iron mask
> The last lighted torch of the century (66).

Wole Soyinka's *A Dance of the Forests* and *Season of Anomie* anticipate Nigerian politics after independence. In 1973, Soyinka told an interviewer: "As a writer I have a special responsibility, because I can smell the reactionary sperm years before the rape takes place" (Streitfeld, 1994:C1). In all cases, by foreseeing terror before it takes place, the writers prepare society for the inevitable problems and challenges that must be confronted for a more humane world.

Writers are builders and healers. With catastrophes and other instances of terror, people are usually traumatized and many suffer emotional and psychiatric problems. It is in the tradition of artists to rebuild from destruction and heal affected people emotionally. In the Jewish tradition of *tikkum olam*, for instance, there is the sense of responsibility to use art to "mend the world." Literature provides hope and inspiration in times of shock and bleak happenings. Literature, especially in the form of poetry, becomes a balm over wounds in times of grief and despair. Generally, writers help to restore society's hope for a better future.

Some writers propose a spiritual panacea to overcome terror. Rainer Maria Rilke's formula is relevant here. To him in 1917, "only through one of the greatest and innermost renovations it has ever gone through will the world be able to save itself" (qtd. in Leishman and Spender 14). And by 1919 he stated that the task of the intellectual/writer in the post-war world would be "to prepare in men's hearts the way for those gentle, mysterious, trembling transformations, from which alone the understandings and harmonies of a serener future will proceed" (14).

The aesthetics of relevance is crucial to the combating of terror in society. No material in a writer's work is extra-literary. The experiences of the individual, society, and humankind form materials and the backdrop of literary creations. The writer should not withdraw into the self and forget the world around. As antennae of society, writers should use their vision to combat evil such as terror and terrorism and make and leave the world better than how he or she met it. Value should be part of beauty. The writer by sticking out his or her head in activism will be advocating the axiom "I do as I write" and thereby gains authenticity for the art.

It is not true that poetry or literature changes nothing. Poems, plays, and novels have rattled dictators in Africa, Europe, and South America. Agents of terror fear literature and the activist lives of writers. They know very well that the pen is mightier than the sword! Jack Mapanje's *Of Chameleons and Gods* unnerved the Board of Censors in Malawi during Kamuzu Banda's dictatorship just as Wole Soyinka's *The Man Died* gave Yakubu Gowon and his military henchmen sleepless nights in Nigeria. If Sani Abacha was not scared, why did he frame and hang Ken Saro-Wiwa, writer and activist for minority and environmental rights of the Niger Delta people? Why did the right-wing Franco forces execute Garcia Lorca? Literature scares and affects perpetrators of evil and terror. We also know the success of the anti-apartheid writing and activism in South Africa.

To the writer, especially the ideologically committed, as Soyinka puts it: "The man dies in all who keep silent in the face of tyranny" (13). George Mangakis thrown into jail by the Greek fascists wrote: "When a dictatorship is imposed on your country, the very first thing you feel...is humiliation...You feel as if your reason and your human status were being deeply insulted every day. And then comes the attempt to impose on you by fear, acceptance of various barbarous actions of theirs that you hear about, or that you actually see them commit against your fellow human beings" (quoted in Soyinka 14). To Soyinka, "the first step towards the dethronement of terror is the deflation of its hypocritical self-righteousness" (15), which writers often do in their various works.

Americans, from reports since September 11, 2001, have become more communal, more society-oriented, and more conscious of the world around and far. Instead of radical individualism, Americans are more and more beginning to see themselves as one human group. In other words, what affects others can also affect me – not just on the anthrax! It is my hope that writers will come out of the cocoon of the self and see humanity as a common bond that society needs to strengthen for the good of all. There is consensus that the world cannot be the same again after September 11, 2001 and I dare say that the world of American literature will not be the same again. After all, literature reflects life.

Terror will continue to ravage the individual, community, and the world if the writer embraces a mere aestheticism that sees style as a literary end by itself. Being a mere stylist is not enough. Literature has been used copiously as a weapon against different forms of terror to affirm humanity.

As has been emphasized, every human being or writer lives in an environment with one form of terror or the other. Terror destroys, dehumanizes, humiliates, and takes away love, beauty, and life. Literature advocates sensitivity and tolerance of others in one world for stability and peace. It is the thesis of which terror is the antithesis. Every human being has a civic responsibility to society and should not be indifferent in the face of terror. We should not leave the fight against all forms of terror to the military and politicians alone. They fight the manifestations of terror. The writer can help eliminate the root cause of terrorism by fighting against repression, marginalization, exploitation, injustice, and many other vices. The writing life, thus, has its responsibilities and in seeking an ideal for humanity, writers in their writing and activism establish a counterpoint to forces of terror and evil and in so doing champion the causes of life, love, and beauty.

References and works cited

Booth, James. *Writers and Politics in Nigeria*, New York: Africana, 1981.
Brutus, Dennis. *A Simple Lust*. London: Heinemann, 1973.
Eagleton, Terry. *Criticism and Ideology: A Study of Marxist Literary Theory*. London: Verso, 1978.
Hodge, Robert. *Literature as Discourse*, Baltimore, Md.: John Hopkins UP, 1990.
Irele, Abiola. *The African Imagination: Literature in Africa and the Black Diaspora*. Oxford/New York: OUP, 2001.
Jameson, Fredric. *The Political Unconscious: Narrative as a Socially Symbolic Act*. Ithaca, NY: Cornell University Press, 1981.
--- "Third World Literature in the Era of Multinational Capitalism," *Social Text*, 5, no. 3 (1986): 65-88.
Macherey, Pierre. Trans. By Geoffrey Walls. *A Theory of Literary Production*. London: Routledge and Keegan Paul, 1978.
Ngugi, wa Thiongo. *Detained: A Writer's Prison Diary*. London: Heinemann, 1981.
---*Devil on the Cross*, London: Heinemann, 1982.
Okigbo, Christopher. *Labyrinths*. London: Heinemann, 1971.
Soyinka, Wole. *The Man Died*. Hammondsworth/New York: Penguin, 1972.
Streitfeld, David. "Exiled Playwright Seeks Sanctions Against Regime," *Washington Post*, Dec. 7, 1994: CI: 3.

XII

Anxieties and hopes: recent African poetry

Critics are so used to African poetry written in the 1960s and early 1970s by such poets as Lenrie Peters, Kofi Awoonor, Wole Soyinka, Christopher Okigbo, J.P. Clark, and Dennis Brutus that they have held back on the poetry written after the mid-1970s to date. Understandably, many scholars would prefer to explore the same turf they are familiar with. However, this attitude sometimes creates a perception that African poetry is either static or dead after that generation of poets. While in other essays I have described the "new African poetry," I intend to survey recent African poetry with a view to noting the major trends that create anxieties and hopes at the same time about the state of African poetry. My focus will be on recent Anglophone African poetry, not only because it is available and accessible but also reflects on many levels all African poetic productions, whether in French or Portuguese, of the past decade. It will take many years for English translations of the recent works of French and Portuguese-speaking African poets to be available.

Certain socio-economic and political happenings in recent times have impacted on the writing and state of poetry in Africa. While there is scope for poets to establish individual voices resulting from private experiences, some general world, continental, and national experiences have a big impact on recent African poetry.

One of the major factors affecting the status of and attitude toward poetry the past decade is the rise and flourishing of literary theory. There have always been theoretical approaches to literature for hundreds of years, but never before in history has theory become so exclusive of poetry in its literary discussion. In contemporary times, theory appears to have demoted or downgraded poetry as a literary genre. While some of the theories such as deconstruction and structuralism still gave room to discussion of poetry, most other theories ranging from post-colonialism to feminism tend to focus more on fiction than any other literary genre. One could say with equal lament that drama suffers a similar fate as poetry. There is the obvious lack of courage and daring on the part of academic critics that are eager to publish to survive in the university for promotion and tenure or acquire academic superstar status not to examine poetry, which needs more rigorous scrutiny than fiction. Poetry is more concise and dense because of its reliance on images and metaphors and is generally perceived as far more difficult than fiction written in prose.

The promotion of fiction at the expense of poetry is reflected in African literature, for instance, in the reduction in number of poetry prizes even as fiction prizes increase. The Commonwealth Poetry Prize has died, even as the Commonwealth Writers' Prize for fiction flourishes. There is even the Caine Prize for African short stories. Also there is the Macmillan Fiction Awards. The Christopher Okigbo All-Africa Poetry Prize has transformed into the All-Africa Okigbo Prize for Literature. These are just a few examples that reflect the downgrading of poetry to the advantage of fiction.

This general emphasis on theory has impacted adversely on African poetry in recent times. At academic conferences such as the African Literature Association's annual conference and the African Studies Association's, academics scrambled to buy books on theory, rather than creative works. The African academics, following the cue of their western colleagues, applied and used (and some parroted) these fashionable theoretical jargons and terminologies. They seem to be using fixed constructs to evaluate literary works and forget that the critic, in a conventional sense, evaluates literary works. So the lack of interest in recent African poetry is a result of the upsurge in the application of theory to fiction. In the past few years though, the interest in theory seems to be waning after its application has been carried to a ridiculous dimension.

Three other related factors in the appraisal of recent African poetry are globalization, the state of the publishing in and outside Africa, and the exile or emigration of many African poets. These factors have varying effects on the production, distribution, and consumption of African poetry. While Africa is part of the world and is open to changes like the rest of the universe, Africa tends to be more changed by others than changing others. Of course, the West comes to mind. Stripped of all its accoutrement, globalization is a euphemism for the westernization or Americanization of the globe. It is an attempt to homogenize the world with western/American lifestyles, values, and image under the guise of free trade, democratization, and others.

The corporate greed that globalization engendered adversely affects the production of poetry by Africans in and outside Africa. No sphere is this more starkly shown than in the publishing industry. Gone are the days when African economies were booming or healthy and multinational publishing houses such as Heinemann, Macmillan, and Longman brought out and distributed in Africa and all over the world so many books of African poetry yearly. In pursuit of profit, these multinationals went through many corporate mergers and take-over and they have all abandoned publishing African poetry. Only Heinemann re-prints a few of their long-published authors on demand through their print-on-demand arrangements. One can say that once in a while a big British company takes an African poetry work not so much for its worth but to exploit the author's reputation. Ben Okri's poetry published in London rode in the cocktails of his successful novel, *The Famished Road*, and his Booker Prize. The abrogation of publishing African poetry by the multinational companies is a big blow to the production of new African poetry since the early 1980s.

The drastic limitation of publishing avenues in and outside Africa for its writers has a negative effect on African poetry in recent times. There is a symbiotic relationship between the poet/writer and the publishing industry. With poets not finding avenues to publish their works, come frustration and the abandoning of writing by those, if encouraged, might have gone on writing good and perhaps great works. Lack of publishing avenues has doused the enthusiasm of many promising young writers.

A consequent effect of the difficulty of publishing poetry is the emergence of self-publishing or vanity publishing in many parts of Africa, especially in Nigeria. The phenomenon that began randomly in the late 1980s has become, in the 1990s and the new century, a universal practice. Doubtless, there should be understanding of poets who want to be read, but the lack of editorial and professional scrutiny of these publications has produced a mass of unreadable poetry books that deserve to be trashed. Often, armed with money, these impatient young poets rush to print their unrevised and immature works to be seen as poets. Such egotistical trips do no good service to the production of poetry in Africa. Only in a few already established voices such as Odia Ofeimun and Femi Osofisan have I seen readable self-published books in recent times.

Many African poets, lacking publishing avenues in their home countries, are forced to publish abroad and have to accept the editorial policies of "others." Since literature is a cultural production, poetry often carries the culture and experiences of a people or society. Foreign editors, usually western, are often ignorant of African aesthetics and judge African poetry by western canons. This often leaves good African poetry as subordinate to English or American poetry no matter its quality or talent of the writer. The topical allusions, symbols, and rhetorical tropes of African poetry appear quaint to outsiders just as those of others appear to Africans. Thus, by not being able to have African poetry published and distributed in Africa, it runs the risk of being not appreciated in its cultural context. Rather it is subjected to foreign, albeit critical, appraisal in the alien environment.

Several related phenomena are also crucial to the fate of poetry in Africa today. Many African poets live and write abroad. While the poetic produce of the wave of African immigrants in Europe and North America in the past two decades needs to be studied more closely, there is no doubt that the poet is influenced by his or her environment and society. While a few African poets abroad may argue that poetry is a mental process and so can preclude the immediate foreign environment and society and still focus on "home," there is bound to be a physical and emotional gap between the immediate residence and the imagined home. Uche Nduka's poetry seems to have lost much of its Africanity the longer he has lived in Holland and Germany in a self-imposed exile. His latest collection of poems *if only the night* shows the damage that exile could wreak on a promising African poet whose earlier *Chiascuro* was strongly anchored on African experience. Many African poets abroad menopause early and become a shadow of their once prolific and vibrant selves. Dennis Brutus has not been poetically productive in the United States; so has been Frank Chipasula. On the other hand, poets like Chimalum Nwankwo and Femi Ojo-Ade, who visit home and reconnect with their roots, are able to maintain a consistent pace in their writing.

Exile and home are common themes of African poets who live abroad. Femi Ojo-Ade has *Exile at Home*, a collection of poems, which relate his experiences in the United States and Brazil to his Nigerian home. Ojo-Ade sees exile as "a dreaded and deadly estate of today's Africans" from the double perspectives of "within" and "outside," none of which offers succour. The writer uses the persona of the returned homeboy in *In the House of Words* to appraise socio-cultural, political, and environmental changes which conflate nostalgia with technological impact, traditional culture with pop culture, and so on.

Of course, American editors publishing African poetry conform to their spelling, punctuation, and grammatical standards often different from those of the poet at home in Africa. Thus, while a few African poets in Europe and North America may be having an airing of their poetry, there is a certain bastardization of their poetic selves so that "others" can read them. This in itself can lead to a form of self-censorship to conform to a type of English that is different from the imagined environment and home that inspire the poet.

Similarly dangerous to the integrity of African poetry is the effort by foreign/western embassies in Africa to interfere with or influence African literary growth and production under the guise of promoting cultural understanding. In Nigeria, the British Council, the Cultural Attaché of the American Embassy, and the German Goethe Institute often invite young Nigerian writers to their grounds for workshops and poetry readings. In the early part of 2004 the British Council started a program of pairing young Nigerian poets/writers with British mentors. The British Council in Uganda as of now (2005) is arranging to bring five British writers and about thirty-five African writers to Uganda for an African literary festival, "Beyond Borders." So capitalizing on Africa's economic plight, the embassies are trying to look good by promoting their own cultures at the expense of the African. A mentor's standards are superior to the apprentice's since the learner takes the teacher as a model. This introduces a very serious type of anxiety into African literature in general and poetry in particular.

The frequent visits of such mentors and the e-mail interaction have raised questions about the necessity for Africanity in the age of globalization. There was a seminar organized by the student writers' association at The University of Lagos, Nigeria, on Wednesday, March 10, 2004 on "Is there need for Africanness in the Age of Globalization?" That one's identity should be debated at all is a sign of anxiety of the young African writer, a trauma that his or her European and American counterpart does not have to suffer. There is gradual erosion of Africanness, as Africans copy values and lifestyles of "others" that hold theirs as touchstones.

There is also an emerging trend of established African poets jumping into the bandwagon of fiction and sometimes drama. Fiction is seen as more popular, more materially rewarding, and easier to publish. Syl Cheney-Coker whose fine poetry has largely been ignored by critics got plenty of exposure in his metamorphosis from poet to novelist. Even though he published four good collections of poetry before *The Last Harmattan of Alusine Dunbar*, it was the novel that exposed him to the world. He currently has two newly written novels with agents. The writer has in recent years started to write fiction and already published a collection of short stories (*God's Medicine Men & Other Stories*) and a first novel, *Sovereign Body* (2004). Similarly, Chimalum Nwankwo whose poetry recently won the Association of Nigerian Authors' prize is working on a novel. The young Chris Abani whose poetry collection, *Kalakuta Republic*, has positive reviews has gone to write *GraceLand* published by the prestigious Farrar, Straus & Giroux. The Malawian poet Frank Chipasula has been working on a novel for some years. Esiaba Irobi, whose early poetry shows much promise, has changed to writing fiction. Niyi Osundare has been writing plays for some time. Poetry's poor sales and lack of popularity are making established poets to abandon the first of the literary genres to seek others to draw attention to their poetry. The African muse must be feeling betrayed!

Anxious as one might be about the state of modern African poetry, there are other phenomena that give hope not only on its survival but also flourishing beyond expectation despite all the odds. The emergence of national poetries is significant. While there is the paradox of national poetries flourishing in the age of globalization, some of the economic measures associated with globalization have led to the abandonment or reduction of publishing African poetry. As a result of the multinational publishers' shunning impoverished Africa, the readership of African poets has been limited to their own nationals because of the small presses that publish the works or just get paid to print them. Nigeria flourishes with such presses. The distribution of poetry works is so poor that many poets often carry along their books to sell personally. Gone are the days when any book published in Africa was accessible almost everywhere. Thirty and more years ago you might be Ghanaian, Nigerian, or South African and easily gain access to works from other countries. Francophone poets such as Leopold Sedar Senghor and Tchicaya U'Tamsi were available in Anglophone countries and vice versa of Anglophone works in francophone countries. The reading public inside Africa has become insular in a way because of Africa's inability to have trade among its nations.

The poets are very mindful of their immediate audience and so write with their immediate societies in mind. One can see the increased use, especially by Ghanaian poets, of local words to have the effect of drawing in the audience/readers to share in and identify with the poetic experience. Kofi Anyidoho and Kojo Laing have done this effectively in their poetry.

On a different level, the focus on the poet's immediate community has led to the type of nationalistic poetry of the Eritrean Reesom Haile in *We Invented the Wheel*. A partisan of the Eritrean war of independence against Ethiopia, Haile fills *We Invented the Wheel* with highly nationalistic and sometimes jingoistic proclamations. One can understand his feelings in the context of struggle, but the reader gets away with the feeling that the poet is too much on one side. "How We Are," "Peace Will Come," "Believe It or Not," "Garden Eritrea," and "Tigrigna" are some of the many poems in the nationalistic vein. These poems strike a patriotic chord among Eritreans.

Closely related to the emergence of national poetries is the attention that contemporary African poets pay to the performance of their poetry. Gone are the days when poetry was an Ivory Tower exercise and only meant for academic readers. The popularity of good performers like Atukwe Okai of Ghana, Akeem Lasisi of Nigeria, and Lesego Rampolokeng of South Africa, among so many others, underscores the importance of the incorporation of oral literature techniques into modern African poetry. This performance quality has made poetry so lively, more communal, and more accessible to the common people of Africa. While one can say that some of the older poets such as Christopher Okigbo in his poems prophesying war and Okot p'Bitek in the Lawino poems displayed performance qualities, these were exceptions rather than the rule in their time. So, as there are poetry jams and performances in the West, so are there also in Africa occasions for poets to perform their works to large crowds. The annual Poetry Africa event organized by the Centre for Creative Arts of the University of KwaZulu-Natal, Durban, South Africa, promotes poetic performance by some of Africa's leading poets.

Many African poets are now very conscious of the performance qualities of their indigenous cultures. For example, Abdul-Rasheed Na'Allah in his *Almajiri* and *Ahmadu Fulani* weaves in many Yoruba and Hausa oral and performance techniques, which enhance his performance of his written poems. He often beats the "talking drum" to punctuate his poetry readings. The African poet thus borrows techniques from the oral tradition to give a chant-like rhythm to the work. There may be globalization, but on another level, the African is reaching to his or her roots to project an African rhythm in the poetry.

A close look at some African poetic works published since 2000 reveals a trend towards a new form of formalism, which has been absent for about two decades. The generation of poets who wrote from the mid-1970s and 1980s seems to have rejected strict form, which it might have viewed as colonial. Thus in most of the poets of that generation such as Jack Mapanje, Kofi Anyidoho, and Niyi Osundare, the form can be described as loose. There was more attention paid to content, which could be seen as at the expense of form. It appears there is a re-thinking on the part of many contemporary African poets to balance form and content.

Chimalum Nwankwo's *The Womb in the Heart* has most of the poems in regular stanzas. Here is the tenth segment of the title poem:

When the red forge is quiet
Under the udala tree

And the nude maidens
Have become sacred avenues

And the spirit children
Have chosen all their mothers

And all the great races
Have been won and lost

And the glow of the moon
Has nothing for our hearts

And we turn our faces
From all faces wizened

And ginger Time descends
In its judges parachute... (15).

Ogaga Ifowodo, a young Nigerian poet, even borrows the English sonnet form to write "Madiba," the title poem of his collection. The poem comprises twenty-seven sonnets that the poet uses to reflect Nelson Mandela's twenty-seven years in prison. The impact of this experiment is yet to be felt but the poet must have at least a technical reason for not modelling his work on many African poetic forms but rather on an old English form. But this again touches on the debate of Africanness and globalization. While the writer has opined that it no longer matters where you live, there is a caveat: be yourself wherever you live!

The writer's recent poetry also follows formal considerations. *Welcoming the Dead* is a neo-epic poem in twenty-four segments and written in three-line and two-line stanzas. *In the House of Words*, for the most part, is based on two-line stanzas. Seitlhoamo Motsapi's poems are also in stanzas, some regular and others irregular. Jack Mapanje's "new poems" seem to pay more attention to form and structure than his earlier ones. Poems such as "It's The Speed That Matters, My Dear Padre" and "On Driving His Political Enemies To Scarborough" are examples of this trend.

One could say of this trend that a balance seems to have been struck in African poetry at last between content and form. This resolves the debate that the Second Generation of African poets emphasized form at the expense of content and that the Third Generation over-emphasized content and ignored form.

A hopeful phenomenon in contemporary African poetry has to do with political changes taking place in the continent. Two examples of such countries are South Africa and Nigeria, the former changing from apartheid to freedom and the latter from military dictatorship to democracy. There appears to be an air of euphoria in South Africa and this permeates the creative sphere. There is abundance of new writing from South Africa and the country's good economy has sustained a good publishing industry. David Philip Press, Kwella Books, and many other publishing houses cater to black and white South African poetry. There is no doubt that the South African poetry scene appears to be the most vibrant in contemporary Africa.

The change from military dictatorship in Nigeria has not yet resulted in a similar euphoria as in South Africa. For one thing there is too much corruption and the democracy is fraught with vote rigging, embezzlement of public funds, poverty, and violence. There are many self-published poets currently in Nigeria and the poems appear not to be of a high quality. While the Nigerians outside might be doing better, it is a sad commentary on the African literary scene with some of its best poets living outside their homes. The Natural and Liquefied Gas Literary Prize administrators have excluded the works of Nigerian writers abroad from being considered for the country's highest literary awards since these émigrés had almost all the prizes in recent years. The point was no longer getting the best collection published by any Nigerian, but excluding the Nigerian writers outside that were perceived to be better than those at home. This lack of competition would lead to mediocrity and the lack of an overall prize in 2004 for fiction has confirmed the cynicism of doubters.

There is cheerful news that poetry is getting revitalized in recent years. Some of the older writers who established the African literary canon have in the past several years published new collections of poetry. Chinua Achebe, better known for his fiction, has recently published *Collected Poems* (2004). J.P. Clark, who has effectively combined poetry and drama, has *A Lot in Paradise* published in the late 1990s just before his play *All for Oil*. Wole Soyinka, the consummate dramatist, has also recently brought out a collection of poems on the markets he had visited worldwide, *Samarkind and Other Markets I Have Known* (2002). These veteran poets are affirming faith in the poetic genre as a most apt and valid medium of expressing the African experience.

A hopeful aspect of contemporary African poetry is the rise of many women poets who now unabashedly express themselves without cultural inhibition. The Egyptian Imam Mirsal currently living in Canada and Mabel Tobrise Evwierhoma of Nigeria, among many others, have written poems that express what it is to be an African woman in their respective societies. Tobrise Evwierhoma has followed up *Poems Out of Hiding* with *A Song as I am*.

A parallel phenomenon is the increase in published love poetry. Male and female poets are no longer shy to expose their intimate feelings as in love poems. There has thus been a gradual self-liberalization that has resulted in uninhibited self-expression. The public has become more tolerant of private experiences.

On the general African poetic landscape, there is diversification of themes as never before. The times of racial/cultural conflicts have passed. The ideological edge of the 1980s seems to have waned and poets express an array of themes as seen in works as diverse as Uche Nduka, Reesom Haile, Lupenga Mphande, Chimalum Nwankwo, and Ogaga Ifowodo. There is a combination of public and private/individual experiences and taken from different perspectives that reflect the complexity of modern African experience.

From the foregoing, the state of African poetry gives the concerned writer or scholar enough to worry about. Many new voices have emerged and many older voices are still vibrant as others long silent broken poetic silence. Thus, in the midst of the anxieties, there is copious hope for a renaissance of the poetry that reflects Africa's changing experience in the age of globalization.

References and works cited

Abani, Chris. *Kalakuta Republic*. London: Saqi Books, 2000.
---. *GraceLand*. New York: Farrar, Straus & Giroux, 2003.
Achebe, Chinua. *Collected Poems*. New York, Anchor, 2004.
Clark-Bekederemo, J.P. *A Lot in Paradise*. Lagos: Malthouse, 1994.
Haile, Reesom. Translated with Charles Cantalupo. *We Invented the Wheel*. Trenton, NJ/Asmara: The Red Sea Press, 2002.
Ifowodo, Ogaga. *Madiba*. Trenton, NJ: Africa World Press, 2003.
Mapanje, Jack. *The Last of the Sweet Bananas: New and Selected Poems*. Highgreen, UK: Bloodaxe, 2004.
Motsapi, Seitlhamo, *Earthstepper/the ocean is very shallow*. Grahamstown, South Africa: Deep South Publishing/ISEA, 2003.
Mphande, Lupenga, *Crackle at Midnight*, Ibadan, Nigeria: Heinemann Ed. Books, 1998.
Na'Allah, Abdul-Rasheed, *Almajiri*, Trenton, NJ: Africa World Press, 2001.
---. *Ahmadu Fulani*. Trenton, NJ: Africa World Press, 2004.
Nduka, Uche, *If only the night*. Amsterdam: Sojourner Press, 2002.
Nwankwo, Chimalum. *The Womb in the Heart & Other Poems*. San Francisco: African Heritage Press, 2002.
Ojaide, Tanure and Tijan M. Sallah. *The New African Poetry: An Anthology*. Boulder, CO: Lynne Rienner, 1998.
---. *In the House of Words*. Lagos: Malthouse Press, 2005.
Ojo-Ade. *Exile at Home*. Ibadan, Nigeria: International Publishers Ltd., 1998.
Rampolokeng, Lesego. *The second chapter*. Berlin: Pantolea Press, 2003.
Soyinka, Wole. *Samarkind and Other Markets I Have Known*. New York: Random House, 2002.

XIII

Inviting the world into the house of words: the writer, his place, people and audience*

1

This is a writer's dream, and blessed is the one who lives to experience it – see the world gather in such a large auditorium as this and also outside to celebrate and discuss one's work! I am overwhelmed by the generous sentiments expressed and the large number of scholars, readers, writers, and others from all over the world. I want to start by paying tribute to my literary elders, the trail-blazers – Chinua Achebe, JP Clark-Bekederemo, Wole Soyinka, and others. I do not forget the oral artists nationwide, including the famous Ogute Otan and Omokomoko Osokpa. Without these literary elders, I would not have been a writer. Dead or alive, they remain my mentors and they inspire me in their different ways to be a verbal artist.

At the same time, I am not the only writer of my generation whose works deserve to be celebrated. Many of my coevals are here; they include Ezenwa-Ohaeto, Sam Ukala, and Tayo Olafioye and I welcome them as colleagues. My good friends Odia Ofeimun, Tess Onwueme, Niyi Osundare, and Femi Osofisan, among many others, have not been able to make it. Let this celebration be the beginning of more attention to a group that has lived for too long in the shadow of their senior generation.

---

* July 8, 2005. This was my statement as the special guest of honour at the first Tanure Ojaide International Conference held at Delta State University, Abraka, Nigeria, from July 7 to 10, 2005.

I have won many literary prizes and been honoured many times for my writing at home and abroad, including at the Commonwealth Office where, together with Chinua Achebe in October 1987, I had lunch with the Queen of Britain and many prime ministers. In Maiduguri, Borno State, the Urhobo Social Club that I was then a member of gave me a very warm reception on winning both the Commonwealth Poetry Prize for the Africa Region and the BBC Arts and Africa Poetry Award. But good as the past honours and acknowledgements had been, nothing compares with this very one – your own people's and readers' recognition of your writing and deeming it relevant enough to invite the world to assemble for a conference in the Niger Delta that has been the focus of my work for the past thirty-five years. Neither an Agbon chieftaincy title nor a Nigerian national honour can give as much fulfilment to me as this conference. Thanks to Professor Onookome Okome of the University of Alberta at Edmonton who not only initiated the idea but worked hard for its realization. Thanks also to Professor G.G. Darah and Sunny Awhefeada who helped to put this together. And thank you all from Botswana, Cameroon, Canada, the United States of America, and from all over Nigeria for your honour in attending this conference.

2

Here where I stand is at the heart of the Niger Delta in which I am deeply rooted. I have repeatedly said that the writer is not an air plant but a human being, who belongs to a place and a period of history. My native village of Okurunoh, after which I titled *Children of Iroko*, is in this Ethiope East Local Government. Okurekpo, where I had my primary school education, is some ten kilometres away. Where I had my first literature class is about five kilometres away – St. George's Grammar School, Obinomba. Also, Federal Government College, Warri, where I took my early steps in writing poems, is about thirty kilometres from here.

It is at this Bareki, the colonial name for Abraka, so-named after the police barracks, that the poem "Abracadabra at Abraka" is based. "Ughelli," perhaps my first political poem, is based on Ughelli, then producing oil and gas but without electricity; what I felt about marginalization as a youth. And Agbarha, "where everybody is king," is also nearby. If you look outside, you will see the lush tropical foliage that in *Delta Blues & Home Songs* speaks the "lingua franca of green."

The sense of time and place makes any literary work relevant. In addition, that sense of place in time also makes the work concrete. The Niger Delta's landscape, images, folklore, and people's concerns all enter my writings. Every writer's native landscape is capable of supplying the human condition to wrestle with. For me, by happy coincidence, it is the Niger Delta that nourished me to what I am. The Niger Delta carries a Pan-Edo culture that involves practices of the Urhobo, Itsekiri, and the Delta Igbo. My symbol of tyranny, Ogiso, is part of the folklore of this large group.

Put simply, I see the world and life through Niger Delta eyes. One needs to be deeply rooted to be strong, and I believe the Niger Delta lights me up for the world. This honour thus takes place in a most fitting setting that gives me fulfilment.

3

Much as I am steeped in the Niger Delta, I am part of the Nigerian nation, which being abroad in no way diminishes. After all, I schooled or worked in Sokoto, Lagos, Ibadan, and Maiduguri. I must have been up to 32 of the 36 states in the country. I spent a good time of my life in Maiduguri, which strengthened my talent, and many poems and the recent "Savannah Suites" arise from that experience. My friends from Borno and Adamawa are testimonies of this bond. I have always loved Jos, the "city in my heart." I have traveled far and lived in the United States for long, but I remain body, mind, heart, and soul Nigerian and African.

Two points I want to make at this juncture. One is the need for a complementary relationship of peoples – no one person, group, or nation has everything; each has strengths and weaknesses and we need to be strengthened by others too. I do not want to be seen as incapable of going beyond my Urhobo ethnic group, my Niger Delta region, my Nigerian nation, and my African race. I am a human being and those things that nurture me can come from not only my home place but any parts of the universe. It is because I am deeply rooted in the Niger Delta that I am a strong Nigerian, proud African, and a determined humanist.

The second point is that in the attempt to benefit from complementary relationships, especially in an age of globalization, one should not always be conceding one's identity and only embracing other people's ways, aesthetics, or lifestyles. One should be rooted deeply enough to also sell oneself to others. There is the need for the local (here the Niger Delta) to be boldly inscribed in the global; hence I will always continue to put the Niger Delta at the forefront of the world in my creative works.

4

The world is changing fast as our culture, society, and environment are also. We therefore have to be flexible and be ready to adapt to the changes. Many of us cannot speak our own languages and do not know the folklore and ways of our people. While we should not cling to the past for the sake of ethnic identity, we have to be selective to retain those aspects that strengthen us and leave behind what is no longer relevant or what is cumbersome.

I am bothered that many artistic and creative traditions of our culture are being destroyed by the blinding zealotry of new foreign religious groups that promote the destruction of our culture. We make fools of ourselves if we say we practice Christianity and so do not have to perform those cultural traditions that in their own ways helped to create a healthy social, moral and ethical ethos in the past. Despite the Pentecostal wave, our people are more devious morally and ethically than at any time before now!

We should be proud of our oral traditions that should be recorded and passed on with new technological tools for future generations. I think of udje song performance that brought the best in artistic and moral achievements that has virtually been abandoned. We need to protect our folklore.

Similarly, we should pay attention to the environment that has been not only our refuge but also the sustainer of our lives. We can see for ourselves the extent of the environmental degradation that has taken place in our area since the early 1960s. We need conscious effort to prevent our environment from being destroyed by greedy oil companies and our own hands. As we cut down trees, we should plant others in their places. We should control our fishing and hunting so that the fish and animals that helped to keep our eco system balanced will not be wiped out in our lifetime. Others are coming after us and we will be condemned for our insensitivity to the fauna and flora that we were unable to sustain for others. We can see that the beans, yams, groundnuts, fish, and game that made us an agricultural and healthy people are gone, even as we have more mouths to fill.

5

Let me go back to my writing. Let this celebration be the beginning of more things to come. As of now I have two major poetry collections and two fiction works that should appear in the next few years. I am therefore not going to sit or rest on my oars because an international conference of this magnitude has held to discuss my writings.

Whom do I write for? I have been studied, read, or quoted by students, scholars, and writers not only in Nigeria but also in Great Britain, the United States of America, Canada, Kenya, Ghana, South Africa, Iran, Malaysia, India, and many other places. I have travelled to read my poetry in over a dozen countries, including The Netherlands, Mexico, Spain, and Israel. I write for whoever reads any of my works, some of which have been translated into Chinese, Dutch, and French.

I started as "a child of iroko" in "the labyrinths of the delta" and attempting "the eagle's vision" in imaginative flights as I sang "the endless song." I had "the daydream of ants" after seeing "the fate of vultures" in Nigerian national politics. In recent times I invoke the "warrior spirit" of Iphri as I sing "in the kingdom of songs." Also, "I want to dance." After presenting "God's medicine men," I accepted a woman as "a sovereign body." I have also viewed "matters of the moment" as "the activist" attempts to change things. As I wait for "the hatching of the cockerel," I also indulge in "water passions and oil remedies."

Now I am building a house of words in the Niger Delta to which all humans are invited. The materials of the building may derive from the Niger Delta landscape and folklore, but the house of words is for all who seek artistic and intellectual fulfilment in art. Above all, this house with local colour is open to all people in pursuit of justice, fairness, equality, freedom, and sensitivity to the plight of the under-privileged. I am against oppression, corruption, dictatorship, lies, dishonesty, and other negative practices that diminish humanity in my Niger Delta home as in Nigeria, Africa, and anywhere in the world.

We are all connected as human beings and should not feel that what happens in one place, however distant, does not affect us. For this reason, we should not stay in our personal refuge and forget about others in their exposed conditions. What happens in Darfur in southern Sudan as what happens in Iraq, Afghanistan, or anywhere else in the world affects us. If we do not stop inhumanity somewhere, it will gradually engulf us wherever we are. We should be our brothers and sisters' keepers!

I write through the prism of the Niger Delta for all humanity. We must not be blinded by love not to be self-critical. We will do injustice to ourselves and the people we love if we excuse them from following the human code of compassion, tolerance, fairness, and justice. In fact, if you read my work carefully, I am more critical of myself and the Niger Delta than the rest of the world – call it tough love, what I practice.

To whom much is given, the adage goes, much is also expected. The Niger Delta, Nigeria, Africa and the world have given me so much – I am truly blessed. I accept your honour as a challenge to work even harder with your inspiration and also to reciprocate the Niger Delta's generosity to me with a gift that will touch the minds of its people. I will be presenting in a moment a copy each of my twenty-four books to Delta State University, Abraka. I also want to honour my commitment to continue endowing the annual Ojaide Poetry Prize for the Delta Branch of the Association of Nigerian Authors.

In conclusion, I want to thank again Professor Okome whose dynamism brought this conference about. Also Professor Darah, Sunny Awhefeada, the Vice Chancellor of Delta State University, Professor Enaohwo, Chief Michael Omeru, and all of you friends, relatives, fellow writers, scholars, and well-wishers. You give me the compelling reason and the divine inspiration to write. I thank you all. I am always, always yours!

Reviews of some published African poetry books

Reesom Haile. Translated with Charles Cantalupo. *We Invented the Wheel*. Trenton, NJ/Asmara. The Red Sea Press. 2002. 243 pages. Price: $21.95. ISBN: 1-56902-163-5.

Reesom Haile's poetry in Tigrigna, a major Eritrean language, grows out of the double heritage of traditional African poetry and modern written poetry. The poet's exposure to the West has contributed to this fine line that he treads and which makes the poetry beautiful. Haile's poetry covers a broad range of subjects and themes, including traditional and modern/contemporary, local and universal/human issues. He covers traditional life in "A Mother's Prayer," "They Raised Us," and "Before the Birth of Toys," among others. There is simple humanism expressed in "Be a Man." Common things like shoes, pen, onion, butter, and parts of the body such as eye and heart are subjects of poems. Similarly, aspects of nature are the source of inspiration in "The Smart Star," "After the Rain," and "Our Path."

Human relationships, man-woman relations, and love are also common themes as in "I love you" and "I love you II." Haile also covers religious themes. In fact, Christianity is a major subject with biblical references lacing the poems. However, perhaps the most important theme in all of Haile's poetry is the political with its nationalistic sentiments. A partisan of the Eritrean war of independence against Ethiopia, Haile fills *We Invented the Wheel* with highly nationalistic and sometimes jingoistic proclamations. One can understand his feelings in the context of struggle, but the reader gets away with the feeling that the poet is too much on one side. Like poets on different sides of the Israeli-Palestinian conflict, Haile (Eritrean) and Gobana (Ethiopian) support their separate countries with equal vigour! "How We Are", "Peace Will Come", "Believe It or Not", "Garden

Eritrea" and "Tigrigna" are some of the many poems in the nationalist vein. "esh" is my favourite political poem.

Haile uses a folk style that is at once simple, concise, axiomatic, and intense. Local sayings and proverbs are common. Many of the poems assume the didacticism of traditional literature. To the poet, "If we share, / We can bear / The worst poverty" (12); hence he condemns greed. Many poems carry a moral edge; others are satirical or just cynical. In "Peace Will Come," for example, the poet asks questions to show his cynicism about peace coming from the USA, the UN, the OAU, or Ethiopia. However, he uses a rhetorical question to reinforce the question, and thus makes Eritrea positive and right: "Where else?" Haile is a poet of simple things and touches our basic instincts; no doubt the reason for the popularity of his poetry among the common people of Eritrea.

Charles Cantalupo writes a detailed essay that makes one understand the context, development, content and form of Haile's poetry. Cantalupo is very knowledgeable in African literature and does a brilliant translation. However, in a few instances, American colloquialisms such as "dude," "cool," "hi," and "Nope" seem to me to have diminished the grace of the poetry.

Reesom Haile has blazed a trail in poetry written in indigenous African languages, and though others have written in Swahili and Yoruba, he has in contemporary times made literature written in an indigenous African language to reach other cultures. Cantalupo's effort at exposing the poetry has paid off. Many writers, following the African Language Literatures Conference in Asmara in January, 2001, are following Haile's lead in writing in their indigenous languages and thus contributing, with Ngugi's persistent advocacy, to the cultural development of their African peoples. *We Invented the Wheel* will remain a unique book in the annals of modern African poetry.

Chimalum Nwankwo. *The Womb in the Heart & Other Poems*. San Francisco and Lagos. African Heritage Press. 2002. 103 pages. Price: Not stated. ISBN 0-9628864-1-6.

Undoubtedly Chimalum Nwankwo's best collection of poetry to date, *The Womb in the Heart & Other Poems* is a major contribution to contemporary African poetry in ideas and craft. Nwankwo appears to be a faithful apostle of Christopher Okigbo—the Nigerian poet who embraced and fought on the secessionist side and died early in the civil war of 1967-70. Nwankwo imbibes Okigbo's incantatory rhythms while disengaging from the obscure allusions. The poetry is simple, highly musical, and enthralling rhythmically. Lines such as "You were alone on my royal seat/Matchless work by nameless genius" (9) appear too imitative of Okigbo's semantic and rhythmic repertory. Though there are many echoes of Okigbo—"moon glow", "passage ways", "colonnades", "labyrinths", "iron dreams", "noon tide", "apocalypse" "calvary", "silences", "iron gates", "thunder", "beach sand", "incense" and others—Nwankwo introduces his own ideas and craft to establish his own voice.

Divided into eight sections, the third and longest section, "Under the Sacred Udala Tree," displays Nwankwo at his best. Tapping on folklore, thanks to his mother's stories, the poet weaves a tapestry of enchanting lines. In the olden days, as told him, marriageable girls danced naked in moonlight under the *udala* tree, where spirit children came to choose their future mothers. The poet creates a surreal atmosphere that reflects the myth and conveys romantically the wholesome and natural life of traditional African culture. The poet deploys metaphors, similes, and symbols to convey his love of the past. The couplets flow like a serene river, while accentuating the tension between spiritual and material values, the past and the present, and natural and artificial dispensations. The title poem "The Womb in the Heart" and "Serene Images" convey the positive life that the poet advocates.

The poet contrasts traditional values with contemporary ones and finds the latter wanting. He unleashes a poetic tirade against the contemporary/modern woman, who seems to have lost connection with the past. In "Lady under the Mango Tree," the subject of the poem appears ignorant of the fact that there was once an *udala* tree where there was now a mango and she has her shop. The woman shopkeeper and the mango tree symbolize commercialism and materialism, which have displaced the sanctity of customs and the spirituality that they involved. The poet calls many so-called educated modern women "charlatans" and is displeased with sexual deviants. The abandonment of old African values causes the poet pain as he finds imported religions, Christianity and Islam, spiritually arid and violent.

The "Cooling Fires" section comprises love poems. The poet laments the "digital rain" of modernity, which turns things upside down especially with untraditional sexual practices. He pleads for a "rebirth" to correct current anomalies. In "That Absence," "The Return," and

"Beach Sand in the Evening," the poet talks of solitude that arises from love. In "The Return," the loved one could be Nigeria, which the poet physically returns to after his sojourn in the United States.

The other sections deal with a variety of themes and concerns. "Volubilis" relates to remains of a Roman town in Morocco, which the poet uses to reflect on the transience of power. Similarly, he reflects on the impact of war on the young in "Rodin in Biafra." He also exposes the civil violations and tyranny of the military elites, who ruled Nigeria for decades with draconian decrees. "Success" is a sarcastic praise-song meant to mock the vulnerability of the rich who share the same humanity with the poor.

The *Womb in the Heart & Other Poems* expresses nostalgia for traditional African values symbolized here by the naked maiden dance under the *udala* tree and the "serene" old people who unflinchingly stood for courage and truth. The poet undoubtedly finds contemporary African lifestyles as practiced by a majority of educated people, especially women and the young, falling short of the spirituality and other virtues of the past. If he is hard on some groups for deviating, it is out of a deep concern for the future of African culture.

One may not agree with the poet's view that he is an "Igbo poet writing in English," a parochial statement that I feel undermines the stature of his fine poetry. However, the other aspects of his poetic theory show experiential and scholarly comprehension of poetics and one who carefully distils ideas into flowing words that not only speak the African and human mind but also enthrals all poetry lovers. The rhythmic flow of the couplets, repetition of lines, recurring images mainly drawn from nature, the tension between old and new, spiritual and material values, and a total symmetry of content and form make *The Womb in the Heart & Other Poems* a great collection.

J. P. Clark. *A Lot from Paradise*. Lagos. Malthouse Press Ltd. 1994. ISBN 9780230505. 45 pages. Price: $7.50.

J. P. Clark has become a worthy veteran of modern African poetry. *A Reed in the Tide* (1965), which contains his earlier published poems of 1963, blazed the trail of his type of poetry. This poetry is set in the riverine Niger Delta area of Nigeria with its rivers, creeks, and lush vegetation from which the poet copiously draws his sensuous images and expresses his feelings and ideas in a lyrical rhythm that has become his poetic trademark. He also sets his plays in this pristine environment of the Niger Delta, a paradise, from works such as *The Raft and Song of a Goat* to the recent Biroroa Plays. Clark is working in a familiar literary terrain in A Lot from Paradise, which marks his return to the land of his nativity whose water, crops, and atmosphere nourished him physically, spiritually, and creatively. In these poems as in his early poems, there is a strong sense of place, a local specificity of the Niger Delta that gives not only local colour but also spiritual colour to the poetry. A few of the poems are inspired by his American sojourn and reflection on the Nigerian military's misuse of power against the poor. Clark fulfils the proverbial saying that "Two hands a man has."

A Lot from Paradise comprises poems of memory, nostalgia, and passion, qualities that enhance lyricism. The poet ruminates on his roots—from the myths of origin of his home place to his relationship with and perception of his family tree of grand-parents, parents, and brothers. This then is a poetic family album that the poet invites the public readership to go through. While he talks about the closeness of the family, he also talks about its problems, including the loss of parents and relations. In both "Two Loves" and "The Last Call," the duality, which is quintessential to Clark's philosophy, emerges—life and death in the former and myth and life in the latter. In "The Last Call," two rivers merge as man and woman full of joy as in spring tide, but have to obey the "last call" of death. There is an element of spirituality when he talks about gifts, which become curses in both "Land of Paradise" and "An Old Man on Trial." It is a paradox that people of the Niger Delta are poor despite their oil-producing land. Clark refers to a founding ritual, in which an Isoko woman had to be sacrificed by being buried to her neck standing and left alone to be fed on by birds of prey till death, a ritual to appease gods to rescind a curse. So there is an elegiac sad tone to many of these poems. Clark draws attention to corruption as roads are contracted out but never made. He also refers to oil spillage, which has damaged the Niger Delta environment.

Clark is very philosophical when he writes on the simple lives of his marginalized Niger Delta people. The poet in wry humour says the dead do not return because they so love their new company. He talks of the mythical tree falling, making a statement about life—humans are bound to die. Even in the American poems, the poet's philosophizing continues. In "A Song of Harlem," he expresses the uncertainty of life despite continuous hope. The poet reminds the reader of the abuse of power in "Maroko," as Colonel Razaki levels an entire shantytown, an action worse than brutal war.

Though a slim collection, *A Lot from Paradise* shows that Clark is far from creative menopause and that he is as strong as ever and even more experienced. He still uses dexterously many of the stylistic qualities that characterize his poetry; here more subtly as he writes like a sage who has seen much of life and can now express his feelings and ideas most appropriately. Clarkian metaphors and similes that have become part of his lavish repertoire of images are here in droves. He uses metaphors ranging from "a ball spinning on its axis" (13), "A house is the flower," (15) to a "harmattan of wet season" (23). It is in similes, however, that Clark relies more on for his use of imagery. Examples include "As commanding Edo's royal court," "like a football," and ". . . years / Rolled like barrels of palm oil" (17). Death is personified when described as "rude." Some poems end by asking a rhetorical question. There is in the poems an intermixture of dialogue, dramatic monologue as in "the Court Beyond," direct address, and use of mask as that of a sage in "Partners": "I looked among the men / And women I know, and I / Couldn't find one couple / That at one time had not / Wished for a change of heart?"(16). What could be simpler and more sage-like than these lines of "Partners"? The poet also exploits the musicality of words in his use of alliteration, assonance, and refrains.

A Lot from Paradise takes J. P. Clark to his Niger Delta home and family roots he is so familiar with. If there is a Niger Delta tradition of writers, as Nigerian critics are beginning to talk about, it is Clark who started it before Ken Saro-Wiwa, Isidore Okpewho, Onookome Okome, and my humble self followed his trail. Here he focuses on his family and the death of parents, and the poems celebrate a great Ijo heritage. He does not forget the plight of his people in the pollution of the environment and the lack of roads in the land that gives Nigeria so much wealth. These poems are simple and carry in unpretentious language the lyricism for which Clark is legendary in African literature. The poems give a sense of place and family and the poet with sophisticated form conveys his feelings of deep roots in a moving manner. *A Lot from Paradise* certainly reinforces the J. P. Clark poetic canon.

Uche Nduka. *if only the night*. **Amsterdam. Sojourner Press. 2002. 154 pages. Price not stated. ISBN 90-806435-2-1**

The poet's fifth poetry collection, *if only the night* demonstrates Uche Nduka's experience in poetic form, craft, and language. The poet, an exile from Nigeria and now sharing residence between Holland and Germany, must be praised for his tenacity in writing in English and apparently living his daily life in other languages. The exile condition of the poet seems to be reflected in themes and style.

Exile naturally draws parallels or contrasts between home and the new refuge. In, for instance, "They Speak of Turquoise," the poet asks, "Do their cock-tail party conversations impress us?" (72). He then goes on to say "Where we're from emotions are healthily voluptuous" (72). There is tension in the exile that flees negative things at home only to experience problems abroad, a condition expressed in "We can't stay. We can't go." The poet thus writes as much about his Nigerian home as about his European refuge. He makes references to Nigerian places and people such as Udi Hills, Ibadan, Lagos, Ife, Nsukka, Fela, and Kris Okotie. At the same time his current post-colonial home informs many poems such as "Aquacade in Amsterdam" and "To You, Dromomaniac." Many poems relate to European pop culture and urban life.

The poet writes about his personal experience. "Two Tongues" sounds like a self-portrait. In the private poems, love is the major theme. There is an element of bitterness in "Music of the Wound," a past love in which "Bisi Daughter of the River/Has become Bisi Mother of a Rover. / She frames me for all the lies of the moon" (48). Much of the love in the collection is physical. It is sad in "Love Unmade Them." However, in "Terraces," the love is exhilarating as the poet invokes the enchanting "flame-haired woman, / garden of my joy" (125).

The persona of a bohemian, unconventional, footloose, and rebellious personality that the poet assumes allows him to use language freely and beautifully. Here and there, the language is rather vulgar but works well in the context of the poet's persona as in "Phallic jocosity / and full-blown cuntitude" (17). In the self-conscious rebellious attitude, he defies norms of decency in "Father, who farts in heaven / Harrowed be thy arse/For crucifying my faxes (96). He calls History "mastubatory" in "Fake of the Flak." Furthermore, there is humour in "The bridegroom was a cow / The bride was a hen" (87). His metaphors are sometimes mixed but always beautiful as of "That white river / at present dresses in mud" (19). Personification is a common poetic tool as of "nights speak to us" (67), the "sky that took a walk / while River Ihme watched" (128), and a "tree growing a beard" (133). There is much variety in the poetic form. Nduka masterfully employs repetition, alliteration, and assonance. His "A Shining Sad Seed" is specifically written for performance at a poetry reading or slam.

Uche Nduka's poetry has matured so considerably that it entertains in every possible way as the unconventional artist strips ideas and feelings of any cover and represents them in a raw authentic voice. The poetry is simple but intense and interesting. Even where the content may be thin, the poetic sophistication rescues the poems and places them in a great height.

Lupenga Mphande. *Crackle at Midnight.* **Ibadan. Heinemann Ed. Books (Nigeria). 1998. 147 pages. $10.00. ISBN: 9781293470.**

If readers (especially African) should come to poetry by way of Lupenga Mphande's *Crackle at Midnight*, they would not complain that poetry is difficult, obscure, dull, and only meant for academics in the ivory tower. Rather they would find poetry a very interesting subject. These mainly romantic poems are simple, witty, and engaging. Mphande's collection has come out at a period when, partly due to publishing problems, African poetry appears to be surrendering its pre-eminence to the short story. The poems are passionate and display maturity of style and skilful thematic exploration.

Most of the poems are inspired by nature; hence subjects include plateau, birds, animals, plants and trees. The poet starts with an aspect of the fauna or flora of his environment as the source of poetic reflection. He expresses nostalgia for the past with its pristine nature as in "Visiting Friends" and "Returning to Thoza." The physical environment is imbued with a rich folklore, which promotes and nurtures the lives of the people of the tradition. While nature is idyllic, there are "war birds" and "bushfires" that presage the coming of modernity with its technology and politics that will adversely affect the people.

Identifying the beauty, solace, and peace of nature with rural environment, the poet complains about modern technology and its destruction of the once pristine place. For instance, in "Along the Rift

Valley," "A few years ago.../villagers rise with dawn, plough/... singing / bracing against morning mist, /making maize fields lush." But

"Now tobacco farmers/mount tractors at noon, rip / the soil sour.../ Puffs of smoke blight through / valley air and drown for ever/love songs of thrushes" (22). The same criticism of destructive technology is made in "The Fig Tree" which used to be not only a "delight to the eye" but a "monument to whoever planted it" and now "the council has voted to cut the tree down / and barter the wood away to tobacco farmers" (44). The poet is sarcastic about development and modernity, which are being imposed on his people at an inhuman cost.

The concern for nature and rural people is carried into modern Malawian politics. He subtly condemns "the tyrant who at a swish of his flywhisk / Mowed people into dust," apparently referring to the late Kamuzu Banda. Similarly, in "Palsied Tyrant," the poet condemns the "palsied tyrant / that scorns his subjects" (87). He condemns all forms of tyranny, oppression, torture, and killings. In a way, modernism with its technology is likened to political tyranny.

Mphande is also interested in people and humanity, hence his very keen sensibility. He paints an indelible portrait of his grandfather, the school bully, a village headman, Maria, Perdita, and others. He uses these portraits to make statements. In the village head, he laments over what has happened over the years. He ranges on the side of the underprivileged as in "We Shall Be at the End."

Closely related to the portraits are love poems. One of the women appears at times to be a muse figure and at other times a real woman—the mysterious nature of the woman adds to the poem's strength. In the other love poems, love is a little distanced and not too personal. Some of the most interesting poems include "Maria's Photograph" and "A Letter to Anjana." The poet will protect his love, even with murder; and he loves her, the more everybody else is against the relationship.

The poems relate to concrete experiences. They are simple but wittingly expressed. Almost every poem is a story that touches on the fate of individuals or the group who have embraced modernity at a high cost for themselves and their environment. The poet is indirectly saying that things could have changed differently, if the people were allowed to carry their past into the present.

Crackle at Midnight is the culmination of Mphande's poetic writing, which dates back to poems in journals and anthologies such as Frank Chipasula's Brothers, Come Home (1987). There is profundity of thematic exploration, which connects the diverse themes of nature, tyranny, modernity, and love. Though he writes from the ivory tower, his poetry is people-oriented. With *Crackle at Midnight*, Mphande has not only enriched the national poetry of Malawi, but also African and contemporary world poetry. This collection will interest every kind of poetry reader.

Chris Abani. ***Kalakuta Republic.*** **London. Saqi Books. 2000. 116 pages. Price: Not stated. ISBN: 0-86356-322-8.**

Maybe because he is relatively young and currently lives in England, Chris Abani is not a familiar name in Nigeria or Nigerian literature. In fact, I did not hear of him even though I was in Nigeria during the years of his first and second spates of imprisonment in 1985 and 1987 respectively. These were years when the Association of Nigerian Authors was very active. It could be because Abani kept secret his time in jail; hence his harrowing plight was not publicized. Be that as it may, his *Kalakuta Republic* is a beautiful work of art out of the tyranny of the Ibrahim Babangida regime in Nigeria. It is always a feat to balance art with suffering to avoid pathos and propaganda, and Abani succeeds in elevating art and humanity above the meanness and inhumanity of tyrannical leaders and their cohorts.

A voracious reader of literature, Abani is familiar with the prison poems of Wole Soyinka and Dennis Brutus that easily come to mind for comparison with his own *Kalakuta Republic*. Most unusual for Nigerian military dictators, who do not read books, Abani's first and second novels might have been so political that they came to the notice of the semi-literate soldiery to throw their writer into jail. Focusing on his incarceration at Kiri Kiri, a maximum security prison in Lagos, Abani with his pen successfully portrays in indelible metaphors and very poignant idiom the tyranny, sadism, and inhumanity of the military dictator and his prison surrogates. While there was the youthful egotistical yearning for fame in being detained, the poet soon found out the harsh reality of imprisonment. He does not focus on why he is in jail nor on the tyrants outside, but on life in *Kalakuta Republic*, the wing of cells in which political prisoners are kept.

The life in jail involves the experience of fellow inmates and the prison officials. The "detainees" used aliases and the speaker of the poems was called Sadam. Of mixed race (Nigerian and British no doubt), he was the "gentleman" though he has his share of senseless torture from the prison officials. Papa Joe, Jeremiah, John James,

Owusu, Okoro, and Peters shared the prison experience at one time or the other with him. While he survived, most of the others died. Jeremiah has for seven years been "on death row, / has not been tried— or formally charged," and yet was 'an infant awaitee' compared to others. The very young John James is kept in place of his father and the pitiful youth dies in jail for no fault of his. Most of the prison guards use very sadistic torture methods and are mindlessly evil. A prisoner wants the suffering to be written in blood, and there is graffiti scrawled with excrement, as the inmates drink their urine, and practice sodomy in the madhouse of Kiri Kiri. Lt. Emile Elejegba is different from the other prison officials who are torturers in his humanity, and that is why he does not last long there. While Lt. Hyacinth Leviticus Nwankwo sacrilegiously extracts confessions with Christian language as he tortures, another official, Hassan, cuts the throat of a dead prisoner to be doubly sure his victim is really dead!

Abani is a very sensitive writer who presents, in spite of gruesome suffering and death around him, the triumph of humanity over tyranny. Tyranny cannot overcome the will and resilience of those who want to overthrow it. He reads even in jail with the connivance of Elejegba. Some of the poems take on a spiritual tone in the Hindu/Buddhist allusions that elevate the persona above his petty tormentors. The poems flow in the mainly two-line or three-line stanzas. The language is witty and carries more of English usage than Nigerian. For instance, the use of words like "obeah" and "coriander" resonates more with the British reader than with the Nigerian. In any case, the collection is full of indelible impressions of characters, experiences/episodes, and strong poetry. "Jacob's Ladder" is my favourite poem:

...Yet you are afraid
to proceed more than a few

steps from the gate. Convinced you
will be shot in the back,

or that people will recoil from you
knowing you carry the stench

of death on your now paler skin.
But nothing happens (97).

The poems after the poet's release as he lives in London show how he continues to be haunted by the prison nightmare.

Chris Abani's *Kalakuta Republic* is a mature testimony of the tyranny and inhumanity of military dictatorship in Nigeria. In indelible lines the poet portrays the experience that haunts him and he calls on all to join together to eliminate any system of government that will perpetrate this sadism of the worst kind.

Index

Abadi/ivwri; 27, 107, 117, 119
Abdullah Ocalan; 128
AbdulRasheed na'Allah; 142, 143
Abku; 25
Abraka; 113, 147
Action Group (AG); 43
Aeroplane; 46
Africa culture today; 4156
African-American; 23, 106, 108, 124
African art; 79
African culture and the new world order; 722
African culture; 19, 15, 21, 24, 43, 45
African Lingua Franca; 5
African literature Association; 136
African literature; 93, 98, 103, 104, 105, 106, 107, 108
African oral literature; 106/prature; 107
African Studies Association; 136
African Writers on African writing, London: Heinemann, 1973; 9
Agbarho; 114
Agbarho river; 46
Agbon clan drums; 51, 52
Agbon; 114
Agha Shahid Ali; 128
Aghughwa (civet cat); 33
Aka; 36, 113
Akeem Lasisi; 141
Akpo; 115
Alan Paton; 103, 109
Alauke (the hunchback); 28
Albert Schweitzer; 8
Alexander Solhzenitsyn; 124
Alexius, 2
Ali Mazrui; 12
Alice Walker; 104

All-Africa Christopher Okigbo Poetry/Literature Price; 82, 136
Almoravides; 55
Amasuoma clan; 113
American Department of Defence's National Security Education program (NSEP); 17
American Disability Act; 49
American English; 101
American literature; 104, 105
Amiri Baraka; 130
Amos Tutuola; 110
Amreghe Grandma; 32, 42
Anglo-French Concorde Jet; 52
Ani (Earth goddess); 27 and lighting
Amos Tutuola; 82, 86
Anti-semitism; 129
Anxieties and hopes: recent African poetry; 135145
Apartheid; 124, 125
Apiapia bird; 33
Aribo Okpan; 67, 72
Aridon (good of memory); 27, 28, 57, 58, 59, 61, 62, 67, 68, 70, 71, 72
Ashanti; 16
Assimilation; 94
Association of Nigerian Authors; 89, 91
Atlantic Powers; 7
Atukwe Okai; 141
Awolowo/Awo; 43
Ayaro Scoopnets; 43
Ayatollah Khomeini; 127
Bakongo; 16
Bamileke; 16
Banla Desh; 127
Baobab Press (Zimbabwe); 4
Bayelsa; 112

Index

Ben Okri ; 4, 109, 137
Benin; 16, 36, 113, 114
Berber; 128
Biafra; 48
Big Brother; 50
Bill Ashcroft
Bill Moyers, 3
Bini; 36, 29
Birago Diop; 8
Birnam woods; 47
Black Arts Movement; 108
Bonny; 33
Booker price, 82, 109, 137
Boris pasternak; 124
Bosnia; 131
Bourdillon; 95
Bradley's "Shakespearan Fragedy"; 47
Britan; 126
British English; 101
Broken English; 30
Bruce Onobrakpeya; 77
Nurrudin Farah; 4, 109
Caine Price for African short stories; 136
Cambridge University; 98
Carl von Clausewitz; 123
Carolina; 47, 52
Catch 22; 50
Celtic culture; 100
Charles Cantaloupo; 152, 153
Charlotte North Carolina; 47, 50
Cheryl A. Wall; 23,
Chevron, 128
Chicago; 51
Chief Jonathan Mrakpor; 59
Chief Michael Omeru; 151
Child labour; 18
Chimalum Nwankwo; 102 ,138, 142, 144, 145 153, 154
Chinua Achebe, 3, 6, 9, 27, 82, 90, 98, 100, 104, 105110, 129, 144, 146, 147
Chinweizu; 87
Chris Abani; 140, 161, 162
Christian Bible; 55

Christianity; 11, 45, 127, 148, 154
Christopher Columbus; 51
Christopher Okigbo; 78, 79, 82, 98, 123, 134, 141
Claude Ake; 15
Claude McKay; 23
CNN; 12, 16, 51
Colonization; 93, 94, 95
Common Wealth literature/poetry prize; 82, 109, 136
Common Wealth Poetry prize; 147
Countering terror in the literary world: the experience of activism; 121, 134
Creative Writer's Club; 99
Cultural imperialism; 21
Cyberspace; 51
Dafetanure; 43
David Philip Press; 143
Davidians; 122
Delta Igbo; 148
Delta State University Abraka; 146
Denning Brutus; 71,124, 125, 130, 134, 135
Derek Walcott; 93
Detroit; 51
Diabetes Type 1; 49
Diabetes Type 2; 49, 50
Diagbe/Uhagwa; 63, 64, 65
Divine mentoring in poetry and its performance; 57, 72
Dr. Frank Eguaroje; 7
Dr. Mc Veigh; 98
Dukana; 128
East African Publishing House (Kenya); 4
East Mecklenburg high school; 48
Eastern Bloc; 13
Ebiegberi, Alagoa; 120
Eboile; 59, 67
Echeha of Ekakapamre; 117
Eda; 25, 49
Edage village; 48
Edjo; 115, 116, 117, 118, 119
Edjophe; 59

Edo; 36, 79, 112, 148
Effurun; 51, 113
Egbesu Boys of the Niger Delta; 122
Egharevba; 113
Egypt; 83
Ekakpamre; 58, 60
Ekaro; 116
Eku Baptist Hospital; 50
Ekverhavwen; 48
Elechi Amadi; 107
Elf; 128
Ematije; 48
Emmanuel Jegede; 112
Emoghware; 96 43
Eni; 61
Epha (bridal) ceremonies; 62
Erhuvwudjayorho fish; 33
Erivwin; 115, 116
ETA of Spain; 122
Ethiope East Local Government; 147
Euro-American culture; 19
European Union; 18
European world capitalists; 47
Expanding the curriculum in American schools – why include Africa literature?; 103111
EzenwaOhaeto; 146
Falstaff NC
Father Cunningham; 98
Fatwa; 127
FBI; 122
Federal Government College, Warri, 98
Femi Ojo Ade; 138, 139, 145
Femi Osofisan; 138, 146
Feminists; 14
Festus Iyayi; 13, 104
Fidelis Overo; 97
Flora Nwapa; 82
Fourth World Conference on Women in Beijing; 14, 18
Frank Chipasula, 2, 138
Fred Will; 46
Frederic James; 134
Frederick Siakpere; 97

Fufu; 94
G. D. Killian; 9
Gabriel Okara; 10, 82
Gaelic culture; 100
Gamalin 20; 33
Garcia Lorca; 86, 130, 132
Gareji (Garage/busstop); 95
Garri; 94
Gary Snyder; 101, 130
Gas flaring; 46
Gateway 2000; 50
General Certification of Education Examination; 93
Geoffrey Chaucer; 98
George Mangakis; 133
George Orwell; 124
Gikuyu; 126
Global village; 51
Globalisation; 84, 106, 131, 136, 137, 139, 140, 142, 143
Gobana; 152
Godiwini (Godwin); 95
Godwin; 32, 95
Gold Coast; 99
Cold War; 13
Grandpa Odjegba; 44
Greek; 55
Gunter Grass; 130
Harlem Renaissance; 108
Harold A. waters; 5
Hausa; 99
Heinemann (Nigeria), 4, 51
Heinemann, 3, 88, 137
Henry Louis Gates; 104
Herzegovina; 131
Hiroshima and Nagasaki; 51
HIV/AIDs; 129
Holocaust; 18
Holide (holidays); 96
Homer; 27
Homi Bhabha; 19
Homophobia; 129
Houphouet – Boigny; 13
Hubbard; 113
Iberian Peninsula; 55

Iboyi (boy); 32, 42, 95
Ibrahim Babangida; 161
Idoma Aliekun; 86
Ife; 16, 36, 112
Igbe; 114
Igbene (snakelike fish); 33
Igbewha of Otokutu; 117
Igbo; 29, 43, 99, 113
Igboduma plant; 62
Ige nets; 43
Ighievwen Polity; 59, 62
Ijo; 27, 44
Ijoland; 33, 50
Ikuku (cook); 95
Iledi (lady); 95
Imam Mirsal; 127, 144
Imoto (motor/car/truck); 95
Indirect rule; 94
Ini-Ede (grandmother mask); 120
International Monetary Fund; 14, 46
International Writing Program; 46, 93
Inviting the world into the house of words: the writer, his place people and audience; 146151
Iowa City; 46, 93
Iphri; 150
Irele Abiola; 110, 121,134
Irish Catholic priest/Reverend fathers – *Ifada*; 95
Irish Republican Army (IRA); 122
Iroko tree; 42, 39, 94, 100
Irorile; 60
Isaac Adaka Boro; 35
Isana (salmon/canned fish); 29, 95
Ishaka; 48, 38
Ishan; 36
Ishmael Reed; 130, 104
Ishoshi (church); 95
Isidore Okpewho; 129
Islam; 11, 12, 127, 128, 154
Isoko; 50, 113
Isukuru (school); 96
Itaba (tobacco); 95
Itisha (teacher); 95
Itsekiri; 27, 44, 114, 148

ITV; 129
Ivar Ivask; 93
Iwhrekan; 59, 63
Izibongo"; 93
J.P. Bekederemo – Clark; 28, 82, 98, 120, 135, 146, 155, 156, 157
Jack Mapanje 2, 3, 132, 142, 143
James Baldwin; 23, 130
James Booth; 134
James Joyce; 100
James W. Moore; 121
Jared Angira; 126
Jebba Bridge; 77
John Keats; 74
John Milton; 55
John S. Mbiti; 10, 107, 111, 120
John W. Robert, 104
Johnson Adjan; 67, 72
Jose Ortega y Gasset; 24
Joseph Conrad, 8, 109
Joseph E. Holloway; 104
Joseph Oderhowho; 97
Joseph; 96
Joyce Cary; 8
Juliana Okoh; 128
Kamiriithu Community Education and Cultural Centre; 126
Kamuzu Banda; 13, 71, 132, 160
Kanchana Ugbabe; 90
Karen Aribisala; 90
Kashmir India; 128
Ken Saro wiwa, 2, 3, 105, 35, 71, 128, 129, 130, 132
Kenya; 99
Kirikiri; 161, 162
Kofi Anyidoho; 141, 142
Kofi Awoonor; 135
Kojo Liang; 141
Kokori; 34
Koku (cork cap); 95
Kolta (coal tar); 95
Kraft Books (Ibadan); 4
Kremlin; 2, 124
Kruman (crewman/sailor)' 29
Kurds; 128

Kwashiorkor;
Kwella Books; 143
Lagos; 112
Leisham and Spender; 132
Lenrie Peters; 135
Leopold Sedar Senghor; 8
Lesego Rampolokeng; 141, 145
Limits; 78
London's Dry Gin; 54
Longman, 3, 88, 137
Los Angeles; 51
Luis Serapiao; 7
Lupenga Mphande; 144, 145, 159
Mabel Tobrise Evwierhoma; 144
Macmillan; 88, 137
Madezhda Mandelstam; 27
Majota; 58
Malthouse Press, 4
Mammy Water; 77
Martin Bernal; 55
Meje (table); 29, 95
Melville Herskovits; 8, 21
Memerume; 59
Mernyeng "SeChan"; 86
Mexico; 55
Michael Foucault; 24
Millikin Univerity; 121
Milton; 100
Miss Poullin; 98
Mobutu Seseseko; 13
Modern African culture; 10
Moors; 55
Morocco; 83
Moses; 96, 43
MOSOP – Movement for the survival of the Ogoni people; 36, 131
Mr Corner; 98
Mudimbe; 32, 24, 26, 37
Mukoro Mowoe; 113
Nadine Godimer; 93, 124
Naguib Mahfouz; 127
National African Museum of the Smithsonian, Institution; 112
National AfroAmerican Museum and Cultural Centre; 103

National Council of Nigeria and Cameroon (NCNC); 43
National Democratic Coalition (NADECO); 125, 131
Nativity and the creative process: the Niger Delta in my poetry; 2240
Nativity; 23, 24
Nawal El Saadawi; 127, 131
Mazisi Kunene; 10, 12, 107, 110
Negritude; 8, 108
Nelson Mandela; 124, 143
Neo-modernist criticism; 5
Neustadt Prize; 89, 109
Neutron Bomb; 52
New World Order; 6, 7, 8, 13, 14, 15, 16, 17, 19, 20, 21, 84, 82
New York; 51
Ngugi Wa Thiongo, 2, 13, 24, 71, 83, 104, 107, 109, 111, 126, 134, 153
Niger Delta Development Corporation (NDDC); 129, 131
NigerDelta 2, 3, 25, 26, 28, 29, 3234, 36, 37, 45, 71, 75, 87, 100, 128, 129, 132, 148150, 155
Nigeria; 2, 99
Nigerian literature in the twenty first century: what direction?; 8291
Nigerian literature; 83, 84, 85, 87, 88, 89, 90, 91
Nikki Giovanni; 130
Niyi Osundare; 102, 109, 140, 142, 146
Nnamdi Azikiwe/Zik of Africa; 43
Nobel Prize, 82, 89, 90, 109
Noma Prize; 82
NTV; 12, 16, 20, 51
OAU; 153
Obaro Ikime; 113, 120
Obinomba, Ukwani; 43, 97, 147
Obo; 33
Obo-ile/Oghwoghwile (Cantor/performer); 58, 59, 60, 62, 67, 70
Odia Ofeimun; 138, 146
Odjelabo; 60, 61

Odysseus Elytis; 130
Odysseus; 39
Ofovwin, war; 59
Ogaga Ifowodo; 143, 145
Ogbanje; 25
Ogbaurhie of Otujevwe; 117
Ogbeyin (the cunning one); 28
Oghighe Plant' 30, 43
Ogiso; 148
Ogoni; 35, 128
Ogoniland; 128
Ogun; 107
Ogute Otan; 69,146
Oil spillage; 46
Ojaide; 30, 120, 146, 151
Oji River; 48
Okigbo; 153, 154
Okitiakpe; 59, 60, 61
Okitipupa; 112
Oko Idon (humming bird); 28
Uhaghwa; 63
Oko-Ibada; 42, 43, 44, 48, 51
Oko-Igberhe; 43, 44, 51
Okot P'Bitek; 10, 11, 141
Okpara Inland; 43
Okpara Waterside; 43, 45
Okpara; 97
Okpogun; 33
Okpoto; 42
Okpreku; 48
Okudo (thick soup for sacrifice); 45
Okumagba layout; 69
Okurekpo; 43, 44, 45, 51
    147
Okwagbe; 54, 59
Ola Rotimi; 82
Old Oyo Kingdom; 10
Old world order; 13
Ologbo; 113
Oloibiri; 33
Olokun; 77
Oloya; 59, 67
Oma; 115, 116, 117, 118
Omokomoko Osokpa; 67, 146
Omowaran; 45

Oniedjo (mother mask); 119, 120
Onitsha; 43
Onyenye first; 33
Ope; 59
Opiri music; 69
Orato (Manlike anthill); 33
Order of the Niger; 90
Orha; 114
Oro (gold); 29, 95
Oroghwuweviya (the one that carries a
    house along); 28
Ororile (poet/composes); 58, 59, 70
Orose (the shell one); 28
Oruru; 58, 67
Osaghae, Eghosa; 120
Oseemo (father of children mask); 120
Osete (plate); 29, 95
Osip Mandelstam, 2, 73, 124, 130
Otota; 42
Othello NC
Otite; 113, 120
Otokutu song; 67
Overe/lilhagwa; 63, 66, 67
Ovid; 27, 76
OvuUghere; 119, 118
Owena; 117
Owhawha; 63
Oyibo; 39, 96, 51
Path of Thunder; 78, 131
Philadelphia; 122
Pidgin English; 5, 32, 29, 30, 87, 97
Pierre Macherey; 134
Placide Tempels; 8, 21
Pollution; 46
Polygamy; 44
Port Harcourt; 34, 36, 29
Post-colonial; 19
Potukri; 29
Prof. Enaohwo; 150
Prof. G. G. Darah; 147, 151
Prof. Onookome Okome; 147, 151
Professor Ayo Banjo; 98
Professor Harold Whitehall; 98, 99
Public Works Department (PWD); 42
Queen city; 47

Queen Idia; 18
Racism; 129, 130
Rainer Maria Rilke; 123, 130, 132
Rape; 129, 131
Reesom Haile; 141, 144, 152, 153
Reviews of some published African poetry book; 152-162
Rherheyere; 117
Rhodesia; 125
River Ethiope; 45, 46
River Niger; 77
Robert Hodge; 121
Rockefeller centre for scholars and Artists, Bellagio, Italy; 92
Romans; 55
Ruth Finnegan, 106, 110
Sabato (shoes); 29, 95
Salman Rushdie; 127, 131
Samarkind and other markets I have known"; 144
Samuel Beckett; 100
Samuel Onosigho; 97
Sani Abacha; 125, 132
Sapele; 29, 45, 46, 113
Sarajevo; 131
Saul Bellow; 93
Scottish Mcveagh; 47
Seamus Heaney; 93, 100
Secrets; 4, 109
Seitlhoamo Motsapi; 143
Self, myth and historical consciousness; on African writer's reflection; 7381
Sexism; 129
Sexual rights; 14
Shangari, 2
Shankari, 2
Sharon Dolin; 5
Sheikh Omar Abdul Rahman; 127
Shell; 128, 129
Shell-BP; 33, 34, 42, 45
Sickle cell anaemia; 42, 49
Sir Juju; 67
Slavery; 50
Solomon Ugbogure; 97

Sonia Sanchez; 130
South Africa Non-Racial Olympic Committee (SANROC); 125, 131
Soviet Union; 13
Spastic paralysis; 47
Spectrum, 4
Spousal abuse; 129
St. Charles Elementary School, Okurekpo; 43
St. George's Grammar School, Obinomba; 97, 147
Stalin; 124
Stalinist Russia, 2, 27
Standard English; 5
Stewart Brown; 5
Stone Age; 46
Streitfeld David, 513, 134
Sunny Awhefeada; 147, 151
Swahili; 126
Sweden; 127
Syl Cheney – Coker; 102, 140
Syracuse, New York; 46
Yambo Ouloguem; 8
Tanure Ojaide; 111, 145
Tarzan; 9
Tayo Olafioye, 146
Tchicaya U' Tamsi; 141
Terror; 130, 129, 121, 122, 126, 133, 134
Terry Eagleton; 134
Tess Onwueme; 146
Tetebe (waterlilies); 33
Texaco; 128
The Activist; 150
The challenges of the African writer today 16
The Guardian (Nigeria) Lagos; 1
The last Harmattan of Alusine Dunbar; 146
The New African Poetry: An Anthology;
Third World; 108, 18
Thompson, Stith; 120
Tijan M. Sallah; 5, 87,102, 145
Tiv "Anzaakaa"; 86

Toni Morrison; 93; 104, 130
Traditional society (African); 9, 10
Turkey; 128
Uche Nduka; 138, 144, 157, 158
Udala; 154
Udjabor; 67
Udje dance song; 33, 30, 57, 58, 59, 60, 61, 62, 63, 67, 70, 71, 72, 93
Udu area; 62
Udu clan; 31
Ughelli; 34, 114
Ughojo (wristwatch/clock); 29, 95
Uhaghwa (god of songs); 27, 28, 57, 58, 59, 61 63, 67, 70, 71, 72
Uhaghwa song; 63, 65
Ujevwen Clan; 31
Ukujere (spoon); 29, 95
Ukwani; 97, 113
Ule Uhagwha R'ive; 64
Umalokun/Olokun (Manny water); 27, 28 goddess of the waters and wealth)
UN; 153
Uncle Onosigho; 45
University of Iowa; 93
University of Alberta, Edmonton; 147
University of Ibadan; 99
University of Kwa Zulu – Natal; 141
University of Oxford; 98
Urhobo "Udje"; 86, 93
Urhobo Folklore and Rhythms; 32
Urhobo; 28, 30 32, 41, 43, 44, 46, 48, 57, 59, 62, 63, 67, 68, 71, 72, 92, 95, 98, 107, 112, 113, 115120, 148
Urhoboland; 115
Urhoro; 25,116, 117
Uto quarter; 58, 60, 61
Uvwiama; 61

Uzerhe; 50
V.S. Naipaul; 127
Vaclav Havel; 130
Vernacular; 97
Viola NC
Virginia slims; 51
W. B. Yeats; 123, 131
Waco, Texas; 122
Walla Walla Washington; 47
Walter Ong; 21, 120
Walter Rodney; 56
Warri; 34, 36, 29, 43, 45, 69, 113
Warren D'Azevedo; 120
Wedlock of the Gods; 107
West African English; 100
West African School Certificate Examination; 97
Western Bloc; 13
Whose English? The African writer and the language issue; 92102
Wilberforce, Ohio; 103
William Faulkner; 23
William Shakespeare; 47, 74, 98, 100
Witchcraft; 49, 50
Woeli (Ghana), 4
Wole Soyinka 2, 3, 10, 11, 27, 7, 1, 75, 77, 78, 82, 90, 91, 93, 98
Wordsworth; 100
World Bank; 14, 46
World Health Organisation; 48
World War 1; 46
Yakubu Gowon; 132
Yoruba "Ijala, Oriki, Rara"; 86, 93
Yoruba; 99,112
Zagzone; 95
Zora Neale Hurston; 23, 37, 104
Zulu Sofola; 82, 107

www.ingramcontent.com/pod-product-compliance
Lightning Source LLC
Chambersburg PA
CBHW011744290426
44113CB00017BA/2650